THE R FACTOR

SCALING YOUR BUSINESS THROUGH MANAGING RELATIONSHIPS

BRIAN L KENT, PHD

The R Factor

ISBN: 978-1-64810-267-7

Published by Perfect Publishing Co.

Printed in the United States of America

ACCOLADES

'BK, in his normal and very predictably easy-to-understand method has broken down the very complex intersection of people and business into easy Tools that are critical to understand in order to achieve success in any endeavor, but especially in an entrepreneurial journey. During my own challenging and rewarding company building journey of nearly 20 years now, I can count on one hand the number of people that have had measurable and direct impact on my outcomes and BK is easily in this short list. The R Factor, importantly with both what is said and how it is said, can become the playbook to success if you understand the strategy and implement the tactics of creating, operating, and building your teams and business as Brian has written for us.'

Timothy Newberry – Founder BlackHorse Solutions

'An executive and manager must read; simple solutions to roadmap the synchronization of people to processes and product. This book is an insightful and powerful look into leveraging relationships (People) to create conditions for success.'

Brigadier General Jeffery L. Underhill, U.S. Army Retired

'BK is the ultimate people person. Having had the opportunity to work with Dr. Kent for over 25 years, I can share with you the reader of "R" Factor is a capital investment in your business tool box.'

Stan Highsmith, Senior Vice President (Industry)

'I have known Brian for over 30 years, and he has always been very insightful. This book is no exception. It focuses on all the areas inside and outside a business and the people in those areas. He keys in on the one resource I have always tried to focus on; PEOPLE and the relationship you have with them.

His philosophy and mine alike has been to take care of your people and they will take care of you!! Some businesses do not take this approach and usually flounder in growing their business.'

Chief Executive Officer, GDT Strategic Solutions Group

"The R Factor" is a testament to Brian Kent's thought leadership and his commitment to helping businesses thrive by prioritizing the power of relationships.'

Gualter Amarelo, Co-Founder of Alchemist Nation

'Kent's expertise in financial management adds a unique dimension to the book, offering readers a comprehensive understanding of the relationship between financial health and overall business success.'

Ron Boling, co-founder of Alchemist Nation

'Brian's engaging writing style and real-world examples make "The R Factor" an accessible and practical resource for leaders at all levels.'

Darina Pogodina

'Brian Kent is not only a man of great vision, but also a man of great action.

I've had the privilege of knowing and working with Brian over many years in my role as a community and economic developer, specifically as CEO of an association of businesses.

Brian emerged early on in our community as an individual of character who brought fresh ideas, calibrated approaches to obstacle resolution, and a resounding "can-do" approach to all he engaged in.

Not only is Brian well-respected former military leader, but his business acumen and willingness to share it across multiple platforms set him apart as a strong community leader.

Whether working together to address complex issues at all levels of government or drilling down into the granular components of business structure, business operations, visioning and beyond, Brian always emerged as a recognized thought leader in each situation.

There is no doubt that this operator and risktaker can help you take your enterprise to the next level and will cheer for your success when it matters most.'

Doug Peters, President, Abilene Chamber of Commerce

DEDICATION

I would like to dedicate this book to my wife, daughter, and business partners, who have pushed me to move forward and do more. They believed I should write this book and share with others the perspective that I share with many around me daily. Thank you, you continue to inspire me to be a better man each day!

ACKNOWLEDGEMENT

There are five men who need to be acknowledged. They have shaped the way I see the world and guided my life's decisions.

John Stone, an amputee and one of the largest farmers in my home county. At an early age he taught me that you don't have to quit because life is hard. You make up your mind to do it and start taking action.

Major General William F Garrison, Retired. He recommended me for my transition to the officer corps, but when I was an NCO in the Army, he instilled in me to make sure everyone knew their tasks and to believe in your people. His motto was: I will support your decision if you can defend it and, in all cases, use your best judgment.

Ralph Osterhout, a friend and someone who is like a brother, helped me make the transition from military life to industry. His mind never stops, and he pushes those around him to never stop thinking. He pushes you to get the education you need; build the road you want to travel and work with folks that are loyal to helping you get there.

Don Johnson, Lieutenant Colonel, Retired. Don has a deep understanding of geopolitical issues, from poverty on the streets to the critical decisions needed to make a real difference in these situations. He is not afraid to say something that nobody wants to hear to get the discussion started.

Lastly, Lyn Berg, business partner and friend. Lyn will be in his late 80s soon and is still vibrant and his mind does not stop. We would sit for hours discussing strategy for logistics, emerging issues and how to solve and fund the items we discovered. I hope to never let my mind grow old nor stop just because society says I should at a certain age. May I continue to think and grow until the Lord is ready for me to move to my next mission.

TABLE OF CONTENTS

PREFACE

For over 30 years, I have watched senior leaders in industry and government make decisions. Some of these decisions have been based on geopolitical problems. Some have been because of market shifts or new restrictions and constraints placed on them.

Over these years and during this time, I have built both my education and experience. I have studied acceptance to new technology and through all of this have realized it is the relationships and the self-efficacy of individuals that make the foundation move. Leaders must embrace this way of thinking. Your employees will rise to the occasion for you.

> "People want leadership, Mr. President, and in the absence of genuine leadership, they'll listen to anyone who steps up to the microphone." Lewis Rothschild, *The American President*

When I left the farm as a young man at the sure and steady age of 17, the one thing I had was a basic education, a solid work ethic and what seems to be lacking a lot today—a grounded version of common sense. I joined the US Army because their commercial slogan then resonated with me:

"Join the Army, it is a great place to start". Being a farmer was not in my future, I had done it, and I knew there was more life out there to do and see.

Now over three decades later, I have been around the world too many times to count and have seen how we in the US do business and how many other countries do it as well. Combining my knowledge, experience and common sense into this book is my goal. You will see some basic analogies along the journey that will make you say, "I knew that." But, as I witness every day in my business life, leaders know it, but they have forgotten to act on it for some reason.

As I work and grow, I continually take courses and classes on what is important to my own growth. I never let the education system tell me which path is important. Taking the path needed for the problems I am experiencing is the whole reason for learning. I never had time off from work for college, however, I completed all my education at night or on weekends. Some people may not want to travel this road, but success comes with some self-sacrifice. I am not saying you must do it my way, but you must make sure you educate yourself. It might be a degree; it might be a certificate program or trade. From where I sit, that is the first step. Your education cannot stop. The systems don't, the evolution in your career field doesn't, so, you can't either!

How to Empower Leadership Through Relationship Management

This book is about leadership, accountability, process, and decision making. However, its primary focus is understanding Relationship Management and its critical role in effective leadership. By the end, you'll have a good grasp of techniques that have proven successful for me and the businesses I've worked with. We'll tackle common issues faced by leaders across different industries and look at how they handle decision-making. We'll also focus on understanding your team's goals and how managing relationships can help achieve them. This includes knowing what your team wants and their aspirations, as well as dealing with the ups and downs of sales and funding. Finally, we'll discuss practical ways to blend relationship management into your leadership style, ensuring you can effectively lead your team in day-to-day operations as well as through scaling your business.

INTRODUCTION

Hi, my name is Brian L Kent. To many of my friends and associates, I'm BK. In my business career of over 30 years and as an accomplished business consultant, I work with industry every day. I see leaders who are struggling or unhappy with their results. Many times, they think their product is about the best product out there. "I have it so they will buy it," is a common mentality. "We wrote the best proposal," business owners say, "so I don't understand why we did not win the bid."

It's a sad fact that many enthusiastic entrepreneurs spend years of their lives building their business, just to watch it gradually crumble before their eyes. Those whose companies are left standing often have problems when they try to scale their business. They've reached a certain plateau but can't seem to get any further. This is what we call "stunted growth." It's like you planted a fruit tree and you believe you have given it the right amount of light, water and nutrients, but it has stopped growing and is only yielding a few pieces of fruit each season. Instead of doing your homework to figure out what the tree needs to grow taller and produce more fruit, you accept it as is and just keep doing what you've been doing. As a leader, entrepreneur and manager, you need to analyze the steps you are taking and ask why your tree is not growing and yielding more fruit. Are you doing the same sort of analysis of your business? Ask yourself:

- How do we measure revenue and staff growth as key indicators?
- Do we have an overemphasis on revenue vs. holistic growth?
- Are we ignoring regulations and lacking accountability?
- What could be some of the root causes of our stunted growth? Consider things like neglecting comprehensive growth measurement, unrealistic growth expectations, employee dissatisfaction impacting progress, or inadequate hiring decisions.
- What are the consequences of our stagnant growth? Could it be having cascading effects on our company trajectory or impacting the overall work environment?
- How do we address growth challenges and identify and analyze root causes?
- How do we set achievable and measurable goals?
- How do we employ thoughtful hiring practices, establish clear accountability throughout policies and enhance employee engagement?
- Lastly, how do we measure success with each thing we change?

If you don't come up with a methodology to figure this out, eventually the stunted tree will potentially stop producing fruit entirely, like many businesses do and have done over the years.

Someone once told me business is a game of relationships. It's about who you know, how you treat your clients, whose office you can walk into unchecked, how you relate with your employees, and how you manage all the relationships within and outside your company. People, in essence, are money.

However, today no one wants to invest the time to build relationships anymore. Today everyone wants to send a 169-character message, a text or forward an email. I want to talk about relationships, standards, and accountability. Of course, we have to build the best product, that is a given. But if we don't do the homework to build a relationship with our vendors, buyers, employees and leadership, what is our market? As the leader of the organization, it's crucial to take responsibility for your decisions, refrain from blaming your team, and most importantly, make timely decisions. Remember, you are the driving force behind your success!

There are other factors, of course, but relationship management is overlooked a lot. This book is meant to prevent you from making the same mistakes that a lot of business owners make. However, I have not written it as a book of just facts. I would prefer not to bore you with the usual business jargon because as a business owner or executive, I would rather tell you the story of one of my clients who had a consultation with me not so long ago. Everyone likes stories, right?

Understanding the 'R' Factor: Nurturing Relationships for Business Success

Business is an ecosystem of many things, but when you drill down to the basics they are Product, Processes and People. The "R" Factor will try to address the People aspect of business. If we look at all three, the one that changes daily and can have the biggest effect on the business is the People and their interaction with the vendors and buyers, each other and, most importantly, themselves. These days, it's common for companies to go through the motions, with managers buried in spreadsheets, trying to predict the future. In our story, Liv's company is in the data analysis business, but we want to discuss the People part of the business. It does not matter what position you have within the company; you have relationships to manage across many spectrums. Executives and managers need to continually know what makes the team tick, so to speak. In doing this they have to understand what is happening with the hundreds of relationships across their team inside and outside of the organization.

Topic #1 Organizational Structure

In building your team, do you have the right people in the right jobs? Relationship Management across your team is important for team dynamics. If you have individuals that can't do the job, their peers look at the individual and ask, "Why is he here?" He or She is not capable of doing this job, they don't have the right skills or they got this job because they are related to the boss. All of these dynamics are important to understand as the leader of a company.

When building your team, ensuring you have the best possible lineup is essential. However, the flip side of continuous team-building is the occasional need for changing players, which is a natural progression. Two crucial aspects here are accountability, ensuring everyone fulfills their duties, and your own role. Your treatment of employees not only during the hiring process but also the support you provide and the way you facilitate transitions plays a significant part in shaping your reputation, particularly for small or mid-sized companies. The prominence of websites like Glassdoor and Google Reviews in business statistics speaks to this reality.

Topic #2 Business Development

In business development, effective relationship management is crucial. In this section, we aim to utilize relationships to scale both our business and our team. It's about more than just customers and markets; it's about understanding individuals. We'll delve into comprehending our customers' challenges, how we engage with them, and the influence of these relationships on decision-making within other organizations. Additionally, we'll explore practical techniques for identifying key personnel and fostering necessary business relationships for our success.

Topic #3 Accountability and Setting Goals

In any business, trust between the team and the company is vital for success. This trust is built by setting clear standards and, most importantly, shared goals that everyone understands and works towards. It's crucial that each person knows the big picture and their role in it. Communicating these goals and tracking progress must be straightforward. Following this, we can set team goals that help build relationships, leading to external partnerships for business growth, or internal relationships that uncover cost savings across different processes.

Topic #4 Effective Management

Once you have laid out the business and set the goals, you can now focus on the external relationships and on how your team can use them for growing your business. We want to use tools that show how the team is fostering relationships and understanding the market better. Where possible, we want to identify how we are enhancing our relationships and how we are drilling into new customers with the same methodology. New customers and vendors have to want to do business with us, that comes with nurturing a kinship and understanding of the people in our team and the common thread we have together.

Topic #5 Communication

Good communication forms the key foundation of all relationships. To truly understand each other, conversations need substance and context. Take cues from books like Gary Chapman's *The 5 Love Languages* to understand how others interpret messages. Building rapport with your employees encourages open communication, whether it's positive or negative. This paves the way for productive discussions to ensure things are going smoothly and for honest feedback during tough times. Applying the same approach across your business processes aids in managing customer relations and understanding their needs, fostering a collaborative environment. It also proves helpful in policy and contract talks, ensuring accuracy through open feedback from both inside and outside the company.

Topic #6 Financial Management

In business, we often overlook the significance of fostering relationships in financial management. Yet, these relationships are just as crucial as those in operations and business development. The team handling forecasting and day-to-day financial tasks must align with the program manager's vision to provide precise data for company planning and external parties like bankers and lenders when necessary. Strong internal and external relationships are key to maintaining healthy cash flow, ensuring the company's stability during both prosperous and challenging periods.

CHAPTER ONE

THE RELATIONSHIP BEGINS

It was early on a Sunday morning when I got Olivia's first email. One of my clients, Todd, had sent an email earlier to introduce us. Her message, much like her personality I would soon discover, was concise and straight to the point. It said that her name was Olivia Lopez, she lived in Tampa and had a small data-analysis and business intelligence company there. I smiled. We could connect in person. She was having problems taking her business to the next level and Todd had told her that I was the person to talk to. She wrapped up by asking if I would be available for a call as soon as possible or if I would prefer email correspondence.

We set our first meeting for Wednesday at a Bob Evans near my place. During a short phone conversation to set up the meeting, I also asked her to read *The E-Myth Revisited,* by Michael Gerber, to prepare her for our meeting. I generally require people to read that book before I meet with them. The concepts and language in that book are enormously helpful and are good to have as a common reference point when we begin our discussions. It turns out that she had read it a few years ago. I asked her to read it again so it would be fresh in her mind. She said she would, we exchanged farewells and I hung up the phone, already feeling keen to meet her.

Coffee & Clarity

I opened the restaurant door that Wednesday morning and was pleased to see that it was almost empty, which was typical for 10am. Most people were at work, so we would have the place to ourselves for an hour or two. I sat by the window so that I could see her as she approached. I heard steps behind me before I even sat down.

"Hi, BK!" the waitress greeted me cheerily. She had a mug in one hand and a pot of coffee in the other.

"Hey there, Sherry. How are you?"

"Oh you know," she said, putting the mug down. She looked tired. "Living the dream." I chuckled. "Are you waiting for someone today?" She asked as she poured the coffee.

"Yes, I am. We'll order as soon as she comes," I said.

"All right, I'll be back then." She smiled her signature smile and walked away to greet other customers who were coming in. Ignoring cream and sugar on the table, I picked the mug up and brought it to my lips. It was too hot to drink just yet, but I liked the smell. I placed the mug back down and looked out of the window.

Olivia's gray Mercedes was just pulling into the parking lot. The corners of my mouth turned up a little as she stepped out of the vehicle and I saw that she was wearing a stylish business suit. *Here is a person who takes their business seriously,* I thought. I looked down at what I was wearing and hoped she wouldn't feel overdressed.

Olivia's eyes found me as soon as she entered the restaurant. I waved her over. Standing up as she approached, I took her outstretched hand. She had a firm grasp, but not too rigid. The word "definitive" entered my head as we shook. Up, down, up, down. Clear, crisp movements that had intention behind them. It was a good handshake.

"It's a pleasure to meet you, Brian. I know your time is valuable, thank you for setting some aside for me," she said warmly, although I could see in her eyes that she was already sizing me up. I liked her immediately.

"Anyone Todd recommends is worth meeting. Thank you for coming, Olivia."

"Oh, please," she said, waving her hand, dismissing the formality, "just call me Liv."

Sherry was already walking over to us and arrived at the table just as we sat down. She greeted us with a smile and handed Olivia a menu.

"Can I get you something to drink to start?" Sherry asked.

"Could I have a coffee and some water?" Liv requested, as she opened up her bag and took out a notebook and pen.

"Coming right up," Sherry said and made her way to the kitchen.

"Let's figure out what we want to order before she comes back," I said.

Liv nodded and looked down at the menu. I did too, as though I didn't already know what I was going to order. It only took her a few seconds to decide. She put the menu down and looked up at me.

"So, I take it this is not your first time here?" She inquired.

"No, it's not," I answered. "My place is just around the corner and the service here is exceptional."

"I hope you don't take this the wrong way," she said with friendly curiosity, "but I thought you would want to meet somewhere, well, fancier."

I laughed. "I prefer a casual atmosphere when I meet potential clients. We're just getting to know each other. Besides," I said, looking around, I like it here."

Sherry brought a tray with water, a mug and a coffee pot. She served Liv the water and the mug, then poured coffee, smiling expectantly at us.

"Are you ready to order?"

I motioned for Liv to order first.

"I'll have the turkey sausage, spinach and mushroom egg white omelet."

Sherry looked at me.

"The usual," I told her.

"So, what's on the agenda for today?" Liv asked, as she blew on her coffee and sipped it, black.

Straight to the point.

"You're ex-military, aren't you?" I asked.

"Excuse me?"

"The way you walked in straight like an arrow, your straight-to-the-point attitude… Even now you are sitting without a bend. It screams military. Marines? Army?"

She laughed. Even her laughter sounded like a woman who enjoys being in control.

"Army."

"Me too," I said.

"No way!"

"Yes," I said, feeling that instant comradery you get with fellow vets. "I served in the Middle East."

Sherry appeared with our orders and set them down in front of us. We thanked her and she flashed another smile at us before taking her leave.

"So, tell me about yourself, Liv."

"Well, I started OBIDA Global a little over four years ago—"

I held up my hand. "Let me stop you there. I want to know more about *you*."

"Oh, okay," she said, a little surprised. She thought for a minute. "Well, my parents came to the mainland from Puerto Rico about forty years ago. They arrived here with very little; just themselves and their ambitions. You know, the usual immigrant story, in search of the American dream. I was born a year or so later, here in Tampa. I grew up working several jobs as a teenager. I really enjoyed it. But mainly, I worked at my folks' store. They owned a local corner store. People from around the neighborhood were in there all the time. Everyone knew everyone. We were a real hub of the community, you know?" she paused, in slight reverie. But it was gone as quickly as it came.

"Let me see what else, I got decent grades in school. I was a bit shy, an introvert, really. I only had a few friends, but we were close. I played on the tennis team in high school, and still really enjoy hitting a ball around the court in my apartment complex whenever I get the chance. Oh! And on the beach, whenever I go there with Umlaut, my black lab."

I chuckled at the name.

"After I graduated, I joined the Army," she continued.

"Why?"

"Honestly, I had no idea where to go or what to do next. Everyone else seemed to have these grand plans but I was more confused than anything. I just figured that the military would be easier until I figured my life out. And I could also learn some useful skills."

"How did that work out for you?"

"Pretty well," she smiled, nodding her head. "I served in Germany, so I am fluent in German. I worked in Logistics, and was pretty good at it. When I finished up my tour I thought about what my next step should be. I always knew I wanted something different for myself, you know? I didn't want to be a worker bee in someone else's hive. I thought about my parents and how they owned a business and were happy doing it, so I thought I should start a business too. But opening a shop wasn't right for me. I wanted something bigger, you know, something scalable. And I wanted to use the skills I learned from the Army."

"Understandably," I commented, as she took a sip of her coffee.

"One of my Army buddies, Steve, said if I started a business, he'd help me. So, I finished up my tour, got a job and used the GI bill to get my MBA at a university where I could do all the coursework online. I worked during the day, studied at night, and I started the business after that. Then, Steve moved from Georgia to help me with it." She took another sip of coffee.

"So, tell me about your company."

"It's a services company. We provide data analytics and business intelligence for our clients. We work on business logistics especially."

"How many employees do you have?"

"A little over Twenty."

"Revenue?"

"We bring in about $4.5 million annually."

"Tell me about your organizational structure."

"My what?"

"The structure of your company. You have twenty employees, right? What do they do?"

"Steve leads Business Development. Our other departments are Operations and Finance."

"It sounds like you're doing pretty well. So, tell me, why am I here?" I asked. "What do you need my help with?"

Her expression changed. She took another sip of coffee, sighed, and leaned back in her chair.

"I'm not sure, exactly. At first, we were a machine. Our revenue shot up to almost $4 million in just the first two years. It was super exciting but then it's like the machine's motor just crapped out," she looked at me quickly, a little embarrassed." Excuse my language. Don't get me wrong. We're not losing money or teetering on the edge of bankruptcy or anything. We're just—" she looked around for a moment, thinking "—stagnant. That's the word. We've stagnated and I don't know why."

I watched her as she spoke. Despite her cool demeanor, I could tell she was more than a little angry at herself.

"The company should be bigger than this," she said matter of factly but at the same time, with an edge. "It's been over four years, and I haven't been able to scale. Then I saw Todd…" she sighed and leaned back in her seat.

"Did you know that we first met at a seminar I attended three years ago?" she asked me, both perplexed and astonished at the same time. "We were both still learning the ropes. Our companies were at roughly the same stage. He was a nervous entrepreneur who had no idea how to get to the next level. Then I saw him last Saturday at the annual Small Business Gala where he won the prize for the Inc 5000 fastest-growing small-business in the United States! *That* is the kind of growth I want. I just don't know how to get there."

"Liv," I said. "You should actually be pretty proud of yourself." She looked at me skeptically. "Do you know how many businesses fail in their first year? You're still here. That's a success. And as far as stagnating, that's what I am here for."

Her shoulders lowered a little. She was loosening up, slightly.

"Tell me about Steve," I asked.

"I owe him a lot," she said quickly, her eyes darting off to the side.

There's something there, I thought.

"Is that so?"

"Yes. When I first told him I wanted to start a business after the Army, he said that he'd help me if I did. And he made good on his word. He joined me and registered for a part-time business course at the same school as me. I wouldn't have been able to get the business up and running if it weren't for him."

I wouldn't have noticed it if I weren't carefully observing her but I could hear tension in her voice. "Why is that?"

"Well, first—the workload. There was a lot to do, so we divided and conquered. But also, we have complementary skills. Steve is one of those people who makes friends everywhere he goes. He's very personable. He loves talking to people and he's good at it. Like I said, I'm a bit of an introvert, so I was happy to let him take care of that part of things. I'm more of a numbers-and-organization-type of person," she explained.

"So," she looked back at me with a small, but proud, smile on her face, "We decided that I would run the business while he would lead sales. He won the first contract that got the company up and running. And they were so impressed with our delivery, that they stuck with us after the terms of the contract ended and started using us in more of their departments."

"But?" I could tell there was a Steve problem. I needed to find out what it was.

She looked away again and sighed. "It's been different these days. The only clients we have are returning ones or whoever they refer to us. Steve says he has it under control but he doesn't. He totally doesn't."

"What makes you say that?" This time, her eyes locked with mine.

"We have bid on more than fifty new projects this year alone," she said in an evenly measured voice that masked what she was really feeling. "But we haven't won a single one. Not one! That doesn't sound like something that's under control. The briefing decks he brings to meetings are all solid. He and the team spend hours, days even, researching the bids and writing out proposals, but it always ends in the same scenario."

"Rejection," I said. I understood completely.

"Yes," she said with a heavy tone.

"That can't be good for the teams' morale."

"Oh, don't even get me started on that."

"What has he been researching?" I smiled.

Even though she was trying to cover it up, she looked deflated. "I think the only reason half the staff hasn't left is because we have some really good people. They are supportive and loyal, but they are also totally frustrated. These days, you would think we run a funeral parlor, not an analysis company. Everyone is demoralized. And Steve just keeps saying that we are fine, but he's burying his head in the sand."

"But you're not fine," I continued the thought for her.I stated simply. She looked directly in my eyes.

"No. We're not fine," she echoed. I could feel her sense of fear and bewilderment in my gut.

"It's okay. We're going to figure this out. I am looking forward to meeting Steve and seeing what's going on with my own eyes." I paused to emphasize my next statement. "I will help you figure this out." The look on her face was tired but relieved and grateful. She knew she wasn't in this alone anymore. It was a good feeling for me, too.

"Okay, looking past the problem with Steve, there's rarely just one reason for a company's stunted growth, so let's take a look at what else is going on." I said as I moved the conversation along. " Difficulty scaling is a common problem but different companies have different reasons for it, it's not a 'one size fits all' kind of thing. Let me go through those reasons and you can point out the ones you think your business is taking a hit from."

"Sounds good," she replied enthusiastically. She picked up her pen and held it at the ready.

Factors Influencing and Root Causes of Stagnation

"The first, and the most obvious issue, could simply be ignorance. A lot of people want to scale their business further, but they just don't know how. Their situation is fine, they're making money, but they can't move forward because they don't know how."

"I have that. Check!" she said, moving her right hand in the air like she was checking a box.

"Which is where someone like me comes in." I said, smiling at her silly gesture." It's my job to show you how to achieve the growth you want by exploring the factors that are impacting that growth. Then, I can offer you a solution or several solutions to get you out of your pickle." I could see her relaxing a bit more.

I continued, "So to effectively talk about growth, we have to know where you are now and then define where you want to be. Those things require metrics and measurement. So, let me ask you, where are you now and how are you measuring your growth?"

Liv looked a little confused. "Well, I thought we already—our annual revenue is around $4.5 million and we have over 20 employees."

"Right. A lot of small-to-mid-sized business owners and, I may hazard to say, most small business owners are like yourself. They don't have an accurate picture of their company because they don't know how to measure growth holistically."

"Holistically?" she asked, her tone laced with genuine curiosity.

I nodded in affirmation. "Yes. People will talk about having a $3 million or $4 million company or they say, 'We have

10, 15, 20 employees.' They're only looking at their top line revenue or they say, 'We're 300 people strong!' But they're excluding very important information because it doesn't conform to the talking points that everyone defaults to when discussing business. It's all fine and swell to say, 'We brought in $4 million,' but what you're not asking yourself is, 'How much of that did we really keep?'" Understanding flickered across Liv's face.

To underline the point, I said, "Think about X."

"The company formerly known as Twitter?" she asked, arching an eyebrow.

"Exactly! They're raking in billions, but they're also losing money every year. So, are they really growing?" I asked, challenging her to think deeper.

Liv tilted her head thoughtfully, "So, you're talking about profits?"

"It's more than just profits." I said, trying to encapsulate the breadth of the issue. "It's almost like net worth. You need to account for both assets and liabilities. How much are we retaining? What are our operational costs? To get a true sense of a company's growth, you need a holistic view."

"Well, I mean," she stuttered, looking a little embarrassed. "It's not like we don't know what our costs are. We keep track of what we're spending for travel and office supplies and things."

"Of course you do," I reassured her. ""But the question is, are you viewing these costs in the grand scheme of things? Are you looking at that holistically? What if the costs go up? Do you know why? For instance, let's say fuel prices go up, and you use Uber a lot. Well, now you have a fuel surcharge, so your travel goes up across the board. Or let's say the gas bill is going up. So now you're stagnating, you don't know why, but you've been ignoring regulations that will have an effect on your company and weren't even aware that certain costs were going up."

Her eyes widened, "Regulations?"

I leaned back, a grin forming, "Ah, one of my favorites. So overlooked. Let me give you a great example. In the 80s the government created new regulations for underground gas tanks that gas stations would have to conform to. But, they gave the gas stations 20 years to do so. As you can imagine, people put it off and put it off. Twenty years came and went and when the deadline to get the tanks up to code came, a lot of gas stations went out of business overnight because they hadn't bothered to do it. Well, this didn't just affect the gas station owners. Most gas stations almost always have some sort of store attached to them. At the very least, they're selling oil and air fresheners. Well now, a bunch of vendors who supplied those stores lost some of their best customers. Had these vendors been aware of those regulations ahead of time they could have planned ahead and found ways to pivot. But now they were going to take a business hit too."

"Whoa. That's not something that would have even occurred to me," she admitted.

I shrugged, "It doesn't to most people. But lack of awareness of a thing doesn't stop someone from being screwed over by it."

"Right."

"The point is, you don't know what you don't know; but you need to know it, so do your research. And regulations and statutes vary from state to state, or county to county, or parish to parish, or municipality to municipality. You need to be clued into anything and everything that could affect your business." Liv's eyes got wider as she took in the deluge of information.

I continued, "And then there's comprehensive growth measurement, which a lot of companies ignore."

"Hold on," Liv interjected, holding up a hand, "How does that differ from holistic growth measurement?"

"You can't just look at general revenue and costs. 'The company is making this and it's costing us that,' doesn't cover it. You have to look at the total company and measure the verticals. Are all the verticals growing?"

I could see Liv mentally connecting the dots, her gaze fixed on the floor as she processed the information. After a moment, she looked up, "So, considering all these factors, how do I set and achieve my growth targets?"

"Let me ask you, Liv, what kind of growth are you looking for?"

"I want to grow one-hundred percent in the next three years and expand nationally." She'd obviously given this a lot of thought.

I let out a breath I didn't realize I'd been holding. "I'm glad you said in the next three years, and not in the next year. One thing many business owners have in common is that they want to build a hundred castles in a single day. That is the biggest challenge entrepreneurs have. They are not patient. They press the lever; they want their tasty treat immediately. They try to do too many things at once. Business does not work that way."

She smiled wryly, "That may sound a bit familiar," she half-joked, sheepishly.

We both laughed. "But your goal is completely realistic," I assured her. She gave a small sigh of relief. "As long as we approach it correctly."

"What does that mean?"

"Well, you can't just go in there and tell everyone, 'We're going to go out and grow one-hundred percent!'" I told her. "You have to break it down. If you go in there with inflated growth metrics, your people know they can't make them. They think, 'We can't do that,' and they just end up ignoring the boss, right?"

"Right," Live replied, her eyes narrowing slightly, processing the information. "So we set realistic goals…"

"But how will you know when you've reached those goals? Or if you're even on the right track?" I challenged her.

"Uhhh…" Her eyes darted around, clearly caught off guard. Her face showed a mix of surprise and uncertainty.

"Don't worry. It's a whole thing." I reassured her. "We'll have to have a big sit down with your team and decide who is responsible for what percentage of the growth and what that means as far as their goals. That leads us into another factor in stagnation."

"Which is?" she prompted

"Accountability." I stressed, leaning forward, slightly. "The only way to hold someone accountable is to be specific with your expectations of them so they know what they should be doing. If you don't have clear metrics and expectations set, then you can't hold your employees accountable to their share of the work. And you'll have no way to see what's working and what's not, so you can course correct if things aren't headed in the right direction."

Liv was silent, I could tell she was reevaluating some things in her head, her pen hovering over her notepad. She took in a deep breath, thinking about what I just shared. "How do you hold your staff members accountable?"

"Let's say I look at you right now and tell you to go to that man's table and harass him," I said pointing at a random man on the other side of the restaurant.

"What?" Her confused look almost made me grin.

"Of course, I'm not telling you to do it." I said quickly. "It's an example. If I tell you to do that, you might just start loudly hurling insults across the restaurant. You may go kneel on the bench in the booth behind him and start flicking his ear. Maybe you sit down next to him,take out a spoon and start eating his food." Liv laughed. "You might even get his phone number and start calling him in the middle of the night or stand outside his house and silently watch him walk from his door to his car every morning. That'd be creepy, right?"

"Definitely creepy," chortled Liv.

"My point is, harassment could mean a lot of things, right?"

"Yes, it could.," she agreed.

"Now imagine I tell you to introduce yourself to him instead. That is a solid goal. If you go over there, tell him your name and then knock his head off, we will have a problem. If you only walk by the table without saying anything, you would have failed in your task. I gave you a clear-cut action to take so I would expect you to achieve it." Liv's laughter had subsided and I could see her really thinking about what I said.

"It is the same with your employees. You need to set clear goals for them if you hope to hold them accountable for what they are supposed to do." Liv was back to scribbling furiously on her notepad.

"Another problem could be employee dissatisfaction. For some owners, it could be a result of an unhealthy work environment. For others, like you, it could be because of the company's stunted growth. There may be a lack of clarity about their roles, or it may be a result of bad hiring decisions. If you have the wrong person in place, what would normally take the right person five hours to do will take the wrong person ten. Whatever the case, frustrated employees can and will significantly impact your progress. Productivity goes down and you could end up having a lot of turnover. Either way, that's money down the drain. Money down the drain is a liability, and when you're looking at your company holistically, you see how all these things could slow growth.

Liv was looking a little overwhelmed, so I relented.

"The point is, there are a million little things that are either causing, or consequences of, your stagnation that you might be ignoring, or not seeing. At some stage you reach a tipping point, where you get all these cascading effects and the next thing you know the company's trajectory is down."

"But then how can I address these million little things if I'm not seeing them?" she asked, looking slightly alarmed.

Diagnosing Growth Stagnation: Looking Beyond the Obvious

"Well, first you have to see them. To do that, you have to get to the root cause of a problem. You have to figure out why something is happening. There's an easy way to do this. Ask 'Why?'"

Liv looked a little surprised, "That seems a bit obvious. If I need to know why something is happening, I ask myself, "Why is this happening?' I haven't been able to figure that out, though. That's why I called you."

"Did you ask yourself five times?"

"Five times?"

"Ask yourself why five times. It's like a little game."

"I don't get it. How would that help?" she asked. "It sounds maddening."

I chucked. "I'm glad you asked. I'll give you an example. This is one of my favorite stories. A local parks and recreation department in North Carolina noticed that there were three statues in the park that they kept having to replace more often than they replaced the others. When they put in for the funding request for the statues the city manager was a bit annoyed, 'This is the third time in as many years. What the hell is going on?'

"Let's say you're the city manager and I'm the guy telling you that we have spent more money on the statues. Just keep asking 'why?' after anything I say. Do it five times." I said.

"All right," Liv said, still puzzled.

I began the scenario, trying to paint a clear picture. "Ma'am, we need to replace those statues on the East side of the park again."

Without hesitation, she played along,"Why?"

I replied, "Because they deteriorate faster than the other statues," I stated.

She leaned in asking again,"Why?"

"Because we clean them more than the other statues," I explained.

"Why?" She asked again.

I continued."Because of the bird residue on them."

She was starting to have fun with it. "Why?" She asked, feigning impatience.

"Because the birds perch on these statues more than the other statues."

She drew in a breath and asked the question one final time,"Why?"

Delivering the punchline, I explained, "Because the lights on that end of the park come on thirty minutes earlier than the rest of the park. All the bugs congregate at the light which means the birds go there too. They eat the bugs, sit on the statues, and leave their droppings there. Which means those statues get cleaned more, so that makes them erode faster, and therefore, they have to be replaced more often."

"Ahhh. Got it," Liv said, nodding. "By the time you get to the fifth "why", you're looking the real problem in the eyes. So, if someone misses their target, ask them why until I find the real cause of the issue."

"Exactly. How would the city manager tell the parks guy to fix the problem?"

"Turn all the lights on at the same time?" she supposed.

"Which is a pretty specific and measurable thing, right? You tell whoever is in charge of the lights to switch them all on at once and either it gets done or it doesn't."

"Right," Liv said, nodding her head in understanding. "Clear expectations for accountability, like we were just talking about." I was happy to see she was connecting the dots so early on in our conversations.

"Another way to look at the challenges you're having is to look at it the way the military might. Evaluate it using the same methodology as an AAR."

Liv's eyes lit up with recognition. "An After Action Report?" she asked eagerly. "Okay, I get that. That's pretty genius, actually."

"Well, thank you very much," I replied.

She leaned in, enthusiastic,"So we take a look at something that happened, and figure out what worked well and what didn't, then figure out how to fix it."

"You got it. Do you remember the specific questions we ask ourselves?" Liv's embarrassed look told me that she didn't. "Just as a refresher, let me go through them for you. The information we are looking for is:

What was supposed to happen?

What happened?

What went according to plan?

What did not go as expected?

What should be changed next time?"

Liv let out an exasperated sigh, "I wish I had thought of that two years ago!"

"But, again, now you know what happened, why it happened and what you're going to do about it. You can give your people clear instructions."

The Power of Transparent Communication

"I imagine that that methodology can also be used to ease some employee dissatisfaction." The wheels were turning again. I was delighted. Working with Liv was going to be fun and exciting. "Sometimes the employee is dissatisfied because something is wrong and they don't know how to fix it. So you need to sit and ask them 'why' right? Then you can come up with goals together."

"Precisely," I smiled. "But the employees can only be happy about having clear goals if you communicate them clearly."

"Why do I have the feeling that this involves more than just saying, 'Dan, get three new clients!'"

"Because it does." I agreed with her. "Better communication isn't just about what you say, it's about who you say it to. If you really want to strengthen communication in your company you need to take the 'one up two down' approach." [1]

At this point Liv had abandoned her omelet and was leaning back in her seat. She folded her hands on the table in

---

[1] Chapter 9

front of her and watched me intently, waiting for me to explain what I meant.

I looked at her forsaken half-full coffee mug, *that's got to be cold by now.* No sooner did the thought flicker across my mind than Sherry showed up with a steaming, fresh pot of coffee, filling up Liv's mug. She looked up at Sherry quickly and smiled.

"Thanks," she said and immediately looked back at me, waiting for me to continue my thought.

I held my hand over my mug before the waitress could pour any into it. "Thanks, Sherry."

"My pleasure, BK," Sherry said and walked away.

"One up two down," Liv prompted me.

I leaned back, taking a deep breath, hoping I could give Liv a clear understanding. "Right. We'll delve deeper later in our talks[2], but think of communication like this: it should flow between you, the person directly under you, and then two levels below that. For instance, let's take Steve as an example. Information should be shared between you, Steve, his immediate subordinates, and their subordinates."

"Okay, so to work on the challenges to our growth, we have to identify root causes, set achievable goals, and enhance

---

[2] Chapter 9

employee engagement," she browsed through her notes, summing up the last few minutes of our conversation in a quick, clipped way. She looked up.

"So, we've been talking a lot about accountability and I get the idea that to hold someone accountable you have to set clear measurable goals and communicate your expectations clearly to them. Let's say you do that, but they still don't meet those expectations. How can you ensure that they do those things?"

"Policies, Liv. You not only need clarity about what you expect but also about the consequences of not meeting those expectations. Think about McDonald's. Their burgers taste the same worldwide. Whether you're in Canada or Thailand, you'll get the exact same burger. This is because of their strict accountability policies. If a franchisee alters anything, they risk losing their license."

"Of course," I continued, "it is much easier to deal with these issues if the relationship between the two parties is a good one. Adversarial relationships always seem to end disastrously."

"So, if we focus on ensuring we have good communication and coordinate with each other regularly, it helps if things go wrong," Liv concluded.

"Definitely. There is also the problem of communication barriers in the company," I said. "Owners are often not on the same page as the managers, or the managers are not properly relaying messages to their teams. Nobody wants to have difficult conversations, so businesses end up dying silent deaths. You should be able to call a manager into your office and say to them, 'Your department sucks. We are planning to cut twenty-five percent of our workforce and I have decided it will be from your department because you are losing us money.' It is a hard conversation, but it must be had."

"I get it," Liv said, nodding thoughtfully, "I mean, I find it really hard to have conversations with Steve about the problem his department is having. I ask him what the problem is, he says everything's all right, and that's pretty much it. I don't know what to say to him or how to approach it."

"You hit the nail on the head," I said. "When you run a company and hire external staff, as well as family and friends, it's important to understand that when they accept a job, they often come with emotional attachments. They may not easily grasp the concept of 'it's just business' because they've joined the team with personal feelings. However, it truly is just business! Failing to communicate this can drive a business right down the tube. It's crucial that everyone you hire understands that you're all working toward the same goal of building the company, fulfilling a mission, and providing a service. It's not like living together in a shared house where eviction feels personal, even though that's how it might seem to them. So, that's why you should make sure they're aware it is 'just business' before bringing them on board."

"You're absolutely right. I know it's the right thing to do, but I find it difficult," she admitted, her gaze fixed on the floor.

"Well, that's why you have me. Communication also means clarifying an employee's role within the company. You can't suddenly get upset with your technician for not selling your product. That's not part of their job description. If you want to involve them in sales, that requires a different conversation altogether."

"I do have a good rapport with my employees," she replied.

"But do they feel the same way about their relationship with you? You mentioned that the work environment has been deteriorating lately. Have any of them approached you with complaints? As a small business owner, do you even have a system in place for them to voice their concerns?"

"Yeah, that's another challenge I'm facing," she sighed.

"We have to fix that," I said, highlighting that the last reason companies stagnate is the problem of retaining talented workers. "A stagnating company often sees its best employees leave first since they have better opportunities. Those left behind aren't always the best to train newcomers. Talented employees need engagement. They're proactive. They'll want to help, to be part of the solution. In sports, it's not just about the paycheck; it's the thrill of victory and camaraderie. Just like in volleyball, every team member has a unique role, but they all need to serve and spike—understand?"

"I don't think that's what our problem is, but I could see it becoming a problem," said Liv. "So what's the answer there?"

"It has been my experience that your talented employees are going to want to have a relationship with you and management. They are going to want to be involved with making those goals happen. Think about it, they didn't become talented in their area by being passive. Most of the time, they will encourage you by wanting to know what they can do to help you get over the net with a win and set up for the next game. When you play a sport it's not always about the money, it's mostly about the wins and relationships. You want the whole package when you are looking for the players. In volleyball, you need each player to be talented at their position, but because they must move around everyone needs to be able to serve and spike—get my drift? They play as a team and when the win comes, they all celebrate no matter who spikes the ball for the winning point."

I looked at Liv, her expression clearly showing that she had absorbed most of what we discussed but was still trying to piece it all together.

I took a sip of my coffee, then set it down, "Liv, let me sum it up in two words for you: Relationship Management."

Liv tilted her head slightly, her brow furrowed. "Relationship management? Isn't that just about how we communicate with others?"

Smiling, I responded, "It's much more than that. Relationship management is the connective tissue between two people. It's a dialogue where you can address any issue, good or bad. It's the kind of communication that allows you to share not just the good things, but also the problems and concerns in a business relationship. Think of it like this: while I may not be the first person you send a picture of your newborn to, if we have a solid relationship, you'd be excited to share it with me."

She leaned forward, intrigued. "So, it's about creating an environment of trust?"

"Exactly," I nodded, "An environment where you can have open communication. For instance, you might talk about casual topics like your dog, the weather, or my recent trips. It's a genuine, free-flowing conversation, not just a question and answer session."

"But what if someone is...difficult?" Liv asked, looking thoughtful.

I paused for a moment, choosing my words carefully. "Sometimes, if you don't have a solid relationship with someone, they might not communicate essential information to you. Like, if there's an operational or financial issue. It's crucial to establish that trust so they feel they can speak up without facing negative consequences."

Liv's eyes widened, "So, in essence, this is about preventing problems by fostering open dialogue."

"Spot on," I said. "For example, if there's a delay with one of your suppliers, and they trust you enough to inform you in advance, you can manage that situation better. If they keep it from you because they fear your reaction, then you're left in the dark, which can disrupt your entire operation."

She nodded, taking it all in. "There's so many ways to communicate now? Emails, texts, social media? How do those come into play?"

I sighed, "We're bombarded with information from all angles. Sometimes, you just need to pick up the phone and have a real conversation. Emails can get lost, misunderstood, or even ignored."

Liv smirked, "I've been guilty of just sending an email and hoping for the best."

I chuckled, "We all have. But relationship management is about taking that extra step. Making sure there's mutual understanding. And sometimes, you need to be able to point out a problem the person is having without being worried you're going to offend someone or damage the relationships. The relationship has to be good enough for you to point out where the other person needs work. You could say, Hey, you might have an ugly baby here.'"

Liv guffawed, "Hey, slap some makeup on that thing!"

I laughed, "Exactly!"I looked down at my watch, "It's been an hour and thirty minutes," I observed. "We've been at it for quite a while." I was conscious not to inundate her with too much information. I had given her a lot to digest.

"It's been an eye-opening session for me. When can we schedule our next meeting?" She was eager to meet again.

"We'll discuss that over email. For now, I suggest you head home or back to work and take some time to think about everything we've discussed today. And one more important thing, please?"

"Yes, Brian?"

"Don't expect this change to happen overnight. I'm good at my job, but I'm not a magician. I don't know any magical spells. It will be hard work and a process, but we'll get through it, okay?"

"Yes, I understand. Thank you," she replied with hope in her voice.

As she stood up, we shook hands again, and she looked me directly in the eyes with a determined expression. She then glanced at Sherry, the waitress, and waved.

Sherry walked over to me and I gave her the tip Liv and I left for her. Sherry said, "Hope you continue to have a great day."

As I left Bob Evans I thought, *It is a fine Wednesday.*

CHAPTER TWO

THERE'S NOTHING YOU KENT DO!

When we met again at Bob Evans, Liv had switched to a blouse and jeans, taking a cue from our last conversation. She sat across from me, fully engaged as I began, "Today I'd like to talk about what makes an effective leader."

"All right," she said. "I'm actually really relieved to be talking about this. Clearly, if I haven't made the progress that I want to, I'm not being as effective a leader as I could be. I'm excited to get started!" she replied, with a mixture of relief and glee.

"As you know, it's the backbone of any business. Without solid leadership, everything's bound to go haywire. Before we dive into growing your company, let's take a look at how you're running the show. Remember that quote, 'I am scared, not of an army of lions led by a sheep...'?"

"'But of an army of sheep led by a lion.' Alexander the Great," Liv completed the line.

"Exactly!" I grinned. "So, let's figure out how to make you the best lion for your team."

"I'm in!" she effervesced.

Leading as an Owner, Not a Doer

"Excellent," I couldn't help but smile at her enthusiasm. "As companies grow bigger, jobs are added, roles are re-defined and some changes in the team's mindsets are needed."

"That makes sense. Like in the E-myth, people have to progress from technician to manager," Liv commented.

"You're one step ahead of me," I said, delighted, impressed by her sharp understanding.

She looked almost proud, her posture straightening a bit. "I've actually read it again, twice, since you asked me to."

It's always such a treat to work with someone so dedicated to growing and learning."Up until this point you've been building the company as you go along. It means that no matter where a person actually fits into the organization, everyone has been building the processes and the product for the business to be successful." Liv nodded her head to show she was following me.

"Well, you've done that. Now you're going to be hiring people. So far you've only needed one, two or maybe three managers. But the next thing you know, you've got ten. And who are your managers going to be?"

She caught on immediately. "The people who have been there and know how things are done. So, now they're teaching others the way we do things."

I pointed my finger for emphasis, "And supervising. Exactly. Because these people have been here helping you from those processes, they know why things are being done a certain way, they know the mistakes that have been made so far and how to avoid them. But until now, most of these people have been on the 'doing' side of things." I could see some sort of excitement building up in Liv. *I wonder what that's about.* "But," I continued, so I could make my point, "they're your technicians, your engineers—and now they have switched into a managerial role and mindset."

"Jim." She blurted out.

"Excuse me?" I asked, laughing at the abruptness of the interjection.

"You're talking about Jim," she stated firmly. "This is the issue I am having with Jim."

"Tell me about Jim," I prompted, genuinely curious.

"He's my Operations Manager," she started. "He is an employee that Steve and I promoted to manage the company's operations, after seeing how hard he works. He always jumps right in whenever there is a problem and he is eager to learn new things."

"Nice. So what's the issue?"

She sighed. "Well, I think there may be a few. The first thing is that he was working with the people he's now in charge of."

"And he has a hard time exercising authority." I finished for her.

"Yes!" she exclaimed. "The other thing is that he is great at operations. That's why we promoted him. But, he struggles to delegate. He's a bit of a perfectionist. Which, don't get me wrong," she added quickly, "I love that he puts everything he has into his work and really cares about it being the absolute best it can be, but when it comes time to train other people, I think he just feels like he can do it faster himself."

I know. "This is a pretty common issue with promoting from within. I always encourage promoting from within, but the person has to step up, make decisions and train the team below him. They have to know they are the manager now and the company can only scale if they can replicate themselves many times to do the job correctly."

"So, I need to have a talk with him."

"Absolutely. He might need a management training class. But for right now, I want to know more about you and your current mindset."

"What do you mean?"

"Well, first let's talk about strategic management—how often do *you* do things because you can get them done better or faster than if you taught someone else to do it?"

"That might be something I do," she said with a smile that let me know that it was *definitely* something she did.

"I'm sure you've heard this before, but as a business owner you need to learn to work on the business, not in it."

"Yes, yes, yes," said Liv. "I know, I know."

"So this *is* an issue for you," I said. "Otherwise you wouldn't be trying to gloss over it."

"I know," she said. "I just…things have to get done and it's quicker if I do them. I don't have to supervise, or correct. Sometimes when I have someone else do it it feels like it actually creates more work for me," she said, looking a bit sheepish.

"Liv, you will never grow your company if you keep doing things that way. Are you going to manage the company as a manager or an owner? You have to shift the way you think about this. Lead and mentor. You can only scale if you train those below you so as the company grows, your vision for the company has to grow. It will no longer be 20 people to lead, but 50 and then 100."

"Okay, this is all fine and good to say." Liv seemed a bit frustrated. "I know this conceptually but when that rubber hits the road I don't really know how to put that concept into practice."

"The way you can do this is to have rules and a plan so that, as the owner, you can focus on growing the business, not just doing day-to-day tasks. This also makes it easier to bring new people on board. Your managers can help you hire more people as you grow. Ideally, you want to promote your current team members to higher positions instead of hiring new people, unless you have to. The key is having a plan for how you want to grow. I know we have talked about hiring and promoting from within, but as the company grows there will be skills and talents that have to be brought in that the current team does not have. It will be important to document these correctly." I paused long enough to give her time to digest this. Then I shifted gears.

"So, as you consider how to bring new people into your business, I need to know how you are balancing product improvement and company growth."

"I hadn't really thought about that." Liv smiled, "I'm too busy improving the product and growing the company."

I laughed out loud. "Yes, I had a feeling. There's so much you're trying to do, but keep in mind that you have to make sure you don't derail the train, pursuing growth." To illustrate my point I gave an example, "Look at the automobile industry. How many times has there been a recall because they shoved a thousand cars through the production lines so they can get more sales, before they realize they screwed up and now they've got to recall a faulty part. You don't want to be the person making that recall."

"Absolutely not!" said Liv.

"It's important to grasp these details not just for the product but also to foster a strong and motivated team. You can't effectively deal with employees unless you understand that they are all different. Yes, they all work for you, but their motivations are different. Their personalities are different, and their talents are different." The look on Liv's face now said *well, duh.*

I continued, "I explained last week, one of the reasons why employees get frustrated is that sometimes you have the right people in the wrong seat. What is your best pitcher doing in your accounting department when they could be out there winning you clients and investors?"

"So how do I make sure I'm not doing that?"

The Balancing Act

I was happy she asked. "To better manage your employees, you should keep the three legs of business in mind."

"The three legs?" Recognition flashed across her face. "Are we talking about entrepreneurs, managers, and technicians?"

"Yes. The three are roles you need to pay attention to when staffing. You, as the owner of the company, are the entrepreneur. You own the business idea, and this meeting is evidence that you try to keep yourself educated as all entrepreneurs should. Steve, Jim and...What's the name of your financial officer?

"Susan."

"Right. Steve, Jim and Susan are your managers. They are with you in company administration. Some people are gifted for that, while others may prefer to be technicians, right? They make the product you sell. But you have to realize that the product isn't the most important thing."

"What?" Liv broke in. She was trying to be cool but I could tell that there had been a lot of frustration building up underneath the surface during our conversation so far. "That makes no sense to me whatsoever. The product is incredibly important to me. It's crucial to me that our services are the best you can find. Weren't you just saying that the product has to be good or we might have to do a recall like the automobile industry?"

"Okay, yes, the product *is* important but you have to remember the other legs of your business." I could see I was losing her. "Business owners make this mistake all the time. They invest all they have into making a perfect product but still end up crashing because they have no means to scale the perfect thing they have produced. Before making a product, you need to consider the cost of production and scaling too."

"So it's the exact opposite of the automobile industry example? I'm confused."

"Look at Apple, for instance. Let's say they want to produce a new iPhone. If they have a billion-dollar budget to produce and distribute this product, they cannot spend $900 million on production alone. They also need to account for logistics and delivery in this budget. You know logistics aren't cheap. The reality is that the new iPhone does not have to be perfect to make money for Apple. It needs to get to the shops and Apple stores around the world for money to come in. If buyers cannot get the new iPhone in the Apple shop nearest to them, or get it shipped expediently, they'll buy a different phone and Apple will make nothing despite creating a perfect iPhone."

At this point, she was just staring at me. Not angrily, but frustrated and with a little bit of disbelief.

I kept going. "Most business owners are focused on delivering the perfect product for their clients, to make sure they always come back. Giving them a good product is important, but not when the cost of production affects your ability to scale. There has to be a balance." I could see that she was comprehending what I was saying.

"So, properly trained technicians-turned-managers will help maintain the balance of product improvement and company growth." Excitement was building as she put it all together.

"Yes, definitely. I once met an entrepreneur who wanted to grow his company, just as you are doing now. His mind was in the right place, but his partner's was not. The guy I met ran the management and sales, and the partner was the technician and was responsible for the product. The partner was all about creating a perfect product. No matter how hard the entrepreneur tried to make the guy see reason, he just would not agree. He thought the buyers would come if their product were good enough."

"What happened?"

"He almost destroyed the company. He dragged them through so much dirt I could taste the mud when we started to rearrange it. The technician side of things is very important, but we *have* to get the product to market. Product and sales need to be synchronized to achieve the best result."

A flicker of understanding flashed on Liv's face. "So, it's not that the product is unimportant, it's that all aspects of the business are. And in order to grow not only does there have to be a balance among the departments but there has to be communication to create and maintain that balance."

I sat back in my seat, impressed. "That's exactly it, Liv, you got it."

"Thank God because I've had to go to the bathroom for the past 20 minutes!" she exclaimed, getting up from the table. "I'll be right back!"

Leading with Vision: Engaging Employees with the Bigger Picture

I considered what we should talk about next as Liv took a quick break. She was very astute and picked up on things quickly. So far that morning, we'd talked about the way the business should work. Now it was time to talk about her role in making the business work.

It was only a few minutes before Liv was settling back into her seat. "Sorry about that," she said, "Okay, so what is next on the agenda?"

"Well, Liv, "I started, "We've talked about shifts in mindset that people in the company have to make. Let's talk more specifically about the shifts you have to make. First, how do you keep things running?"

"I'm not sure what you mean," she said.

"I mean how do you keep your employees involved and motivated?" I asked.

"Well…" she gave it some thought. "When it's someone's birthday, we have cake."

I guffawed. "Food is a very good motivator, it's true. As is celebration and recognition. But those are like boosts. I'm talking about long-term consistent motivation."

"I pay them?" Her reply was almost a question, as her voice

went up at the end, knowing it wasn't the answer I was looking for but it was what she could think of at the moment.

"You have to tell your employees about the mission. You need them to have buy-in. Everyone else should know your dreams and vision for the company. Your employees should be able to recite your company's mission and vision in their sleep. Do you know how the Navy trains their SEALs?"

"I've heard a little about their training," she answered.

"These guys are some of the hardest soldiers in the world. Their attrition rate is extremely high. The goal of most of their training cycle is to get as many candidates as possible to give up. During their training, they have this exercise where their instructors just throw them a heavy bag and tell them to march without informing them how far they are supposed to go. They just say, 'Hey, pick up this bag and start running.'"

"That's it?" she asked, "Just 'run'?"

"When you don't know your destination, the journey seems longer. It is the same situation you are putting your employees in if they do not know your vision for the business. You are just telling them, 'Hey, come to work every day. Just keep typing those letters and sending those bids.' The result is that they start to wonder about the necessity of whatever they are doing in the first place. Then you get work done half-heartedly. Employees also start slacking off because they do not see the point of anything they are doing."

"That's exactly what I've done!" she exclaimed. "They don't see a point in what they're doing. They don't think we're helping people. They're just doing a task they don't really see a point to. They don't know how they fit into the larger plan and why we're doing what we do in the first place."

"You need to align them with your vision.[3] It is your job to have a vision. It is their job to help you realize it. How can they work towards something they don't even know about?"

"So what's the best way of going about this?"

"You have to do more than tell them. If that's all you do, they'll forget. It needs to be deeply ingrained in the company culture. Put it everywhere. Let them see the vision around the office. It is key that all your subordinates and your peers know which direction you are heading so that everyone can keep rowing in that same direction. It will remind them that the company has a purpose, and they all have a role in that purpose. By establishing clear role definitions, you create a framework that guides their actions in line with the company's vision."

The Art of Empowered Decision-Making

"Another potential minefield is in the area of decision making," I said, taking a sip of my coffee.

[3] Chapter 7

"I get that. That's one of the hardest parts of my job," Liv stated as though she was getting tired just thinking about it.

"It is the most daunting task you will ever have to undertake as a leader," I began, trying to connect with her on an even deeper level. "Why are Generals more respected and paid better than Captains? It is because of the different decisions they must make and how impactful those decisions will be. It is why the POTUS is in a delicate position. The President is responsible for making decisions that will shape history and change the world. You are the POTUS of your company. The decisions you make, or do not make, will affect the life of everyone working for you and the business itself."

She hesitated slightly,"The decisions I do not make?"

I leaned in, hoping to emphasize the gravity of an action,"Lack of decision is also a decision. You have decided not to make a decision, right?"

"Right," she nodded. "But how can I know I'm making the right decision?"

"If I knew the secret to that, I would be the richest person in the world. The CEOs of global industries would happily give half of what they have for the ability to make the right decisions all the time. Don't be mistaken. There is a risk in every decision, even if it's just a little one. You can only hope to make good decisions based on the data you have, the snapshot time, the information you are given, and your risk tolerance level."

I could see her working to fit all the information into place in her mind. To help her do this I went on, "Leadership is a business of risk, but decisions have to be made. It is how companies run. If you do not decide, you are delegating the decision-making process to someone else. Your lack of decision would force your employees to make one on your behalf."

Liv made a face. "I definitely don't want that."

"If any tragedy strikes because someone else makes a bad decision, it's still on you. It'll be your fault because you refused to own your responsibility. You refused to own the company," I said. "So now you may not be getting what you want, but you didn't make the decision, so you get what you get."

She sounded a little fatigued. "But there are so many decisions to be made and honestly, I might not be the best qualified in the company to make them. If it has to do with someone else's specialty, should I really be making every single decision? That's just exhausting."

I nodded, acknowledging her point,"You're right, Liv. You can't think about everything, can you? You can't scale if everything's got to come back to the owner. The key lies in knowing who makes what decisions. This is about empowering your employees, but it's critical to define the boundaries of their power very clearly.

"Letting your employees know where their decision making authority stops and starts is critical. Lay out clear guidance to your employees. For instance, maybe they can't hire and fire. Maybe only *you* can hire or fire someone. If you let others fire people, there can be a lot of complicated implications for things like employment security commission and others. You don't want some manager just flying off the handle and throwing someone out of the building. Then you've got a bunch of paperwork you have to do or even lawsuits."

I shrugged, "In the end, Liv, it's your decision, your responsibility. You have to delegate the decision making so that all of your subordinates know who can make what decisions on your behalf. Some people you can trust and some you can't."

"We definitely want to avoid those," she interjected.

"So, how do I know when I should be making the decision and when I should leave it to the managers?"

"I recommend using an Authority Matrix," I began, aiming to provide her with a practical solution. "It's how you divide your decision-making process according to who has the authority to make what decisions. That is why companies have a department in charge of finances and one in charge of accounting for those finances. There is a department in charge of sales and another in charge of marketing. The department in charge of acquisitions is different from the one in charge of production.

"It is also how you determine who has the authority to sign for what. It is how you ensure the right flow of power in your company. If you need a new lease for your company in Hawaii, for example, a technician in Florida should not be able to sign off on it. Whoever was signing it wouldn't know if there were things in the document that needed to be changed. It's just one technician with an itchy pen."

"That makes sense," Liv said.

I nodded in agreement. "There should be a flow of authority from you to where you want the authority to end. Who do you want responsible for the final say on which things in your company?"

"So, it separates the regular worker from the decision-makers?" she pondered.

"Yes. Then, among the decision makers, it separates who can decide what on a given subject. If you already have a schedule for delivering a product, your manager should not be able to sign off on something that says the schedule should be shifted. A shifted schedule means you will go over budget and have to take from your reserves. The decision should rest with you since it is your money that will be spent to shift it." I could tell that had hit home for Liv.

"Split the authority across departments as appropriate. A document could pass from your contracts officer to your program manager for review, then to your vice president of production for authorization, and finally, the senior contract manager would sign, but only after everyone else has had an opportunity to review it for correctness. It's about ensuring decisions are appropriately staffed with all involved. This will help you to create a structure that maintains control."

"What if it's not set up correctly?"

I sighed, recalling a past experience. "I once collaborated with a company that overlooked their matrix. An engineer made an erroneous change order, costing them $25,000 in unnecessary products."

"Oh my God!" Olivia exclaimed.

Emphasizing my point, I continued, "Without proper processes, one wrong move can lead to legal battles, ruined reputations, and huge financial losses. That being said, you shouldn't be making every call. Why hire managers if they don't contribute?

"For every meeting set up to address a problem a manager brings you, they should bring you multiple solutions. If you must come up with all of the solutions and make every decision on your own, then why did you need them?" I drained the last of my coffee and set the mug down with a light clink. Olivia straightened up and collected her notes.

"Brian," she began, gratitude evident in her voice, "this has been immensely helpful. I have a lot to consider and implement. It's overwhelming, but it's also empowering."

I smiled warmly. "Liv, every leader feels overwhelmed at times. Just remember, you've got the right mindset and the will to adapt and learn. That's more than half the battle."

She chuckled, "And a good mentor."

We both stood, I pulled out my wallet. "It's on me," I said, signaling to Sherry. Olivia began to protest, but I raised a hand. "Consider it an investment in the future of your company."

She smiled, touched by the gesture. "Thank you, Brian."

We walked out of the restaurant, both headed to the parking lot.

"As much as I've learned from our chat," Olivia said, breaking the comfortable silence between them, "I've realized I need to trust my team more and create a system that empowers everyone."

I nodded, "Your challenges will only illuminate your path forward. Trust in yourself, your team, and the processes you'll put in place."

Olivia took a deep breath, "I will."

I grinned, "Let's put something on the books for a couple weeks from now."

She nodded, "Sure, I'll get in touch with your assistant."

"Great. Keep me updated. Take care, Liv."

"You too!" She waved cheerily as she headed off to her car.

As I walked to the truck and got in, I was lost in thought about the morning's fruitful discussion. There were challenges ahead but I looked forward to guiding Liv through them.

CHAPTER THREE
INSIDE THE MACHINE

Pulling into the office complex four weeks later, I parked and looked at the array of buildings before me. Before stepping out of the truck, I took a moment to pack my notes. I adjusted my suit and proceeded to enter the building.

When I arrived at OBIDA Global's suite, the glass door had the company's name etched on it. As I opened the door and stepped into the reception area I could see that the space was professional and inviting, with a clear effort to impress clients right from the start. There was a soft, trickling sound issued from the wall-mounted water feature behind the reception desk. I love a good water feature.

The receptionist was a pleasant, well-dressed young lady with a bubbly energy.

"You must be Mr. Kent!" she said smiling.

"I am!" *They know how to make you feel welcome here,* I thought. "But you can call me BK."

"I'm Kerry. Have a seat. I'll let her know you're here." She picked up the phone, pressed a button and said, "Mr. Kent is here." After she hung up, she turned back to me and asked, "Can I get you coffee or some water?"

"Water would be great." Kerry went around the corner, and quickly came back with a bottle of water. As she was handing it to me, Olivia came down the hall.

"Brian!" Oliva greeted me with delight. She stretched her hand to me as I stood up to take it. "I am so glad you could make it."

I shook her hand and answered, "My pleasure." I turned back to Kerry, "Nice to meet you!"

"Please come in," Liv said as she ushered me down the hall, past some cubicles. I looked over at them as we went by. People were in their seats, in front of their computers, tapping away or on the phone. It looked like they went about their business efficiently, but you could see in a lot of their faces that they were somewhere else. I continued following Liv into her office.

It was everything I'd anticipated it would be. It was modest, yet it subtly showcased her achievements. Her accolades tastefully adorned the walls, interspersed with personal touches like family photos and some pictures of local community events she was obviously proud to be involved with.

"Your office is very neatly groomed, Liv," I commented appreciatively, glancing at the organized piles on her desk.

She smiled, "I like to keep things in order."

We settled into our chairs. "All right then, who will be in the room?" I asked. Liv leaned back, "Steve and Jim are there and Susan from Finance will be joining us."

"Before we go in, have you set any expectations about what we are doing today?"

She shrugged slightly, "Just the basics, that you're here to help us refine our processes and strategize to move past this plateau we seem to have hit."

"Well, let's get to it, then." And with that we got up and walked down the hall and into the conference room.

Introduction to the Team

Steve, Jim, and Susan were already in the conference room. As we entered, the team stood up and came forward to greet me.

Liv introduced me, "Everyone, this is Brian."

Starting with Steve, I extended my hand. He took it in a firm grasp. I noted the look of cautious optimism in his eyes. "Brian," he acknowledged, nodding slightly.

"Steve," I replied.

Next was Jim. His handshake was enthusiastic, his grip strong. "Glad you're here," he said, the corners of his eyes crinkling with genuine pleasure. I got the sense that Jim was someone ever-eager to learn and absorb. Someone with a sponge mentality.

Then there was Susan. She reached out her hand to shake mine. Her handshake was a bit timid. She was clearly an introvert. "Thanks for coming," she said, smiling nervously.

Liv took her seat, indicating for me to sit beside her. The room's ambiance was professional with everyone anticipating the unfolding meeting.

Wanting to get a clearer picture of the team before diving deep, I started, "Thank you for having me. I'm excited to be here. I have heard a lot about you and am looking forward to getting to know you better. So, I'd like to take a minute and go around the room and have everyone tell me what they do." This was one of my favorite parts. Asking people what they think they do and seeing how that contrasts with what they actually do.

Steve leaned forward slightly, exuding a mixture of pride and professionalism. "I'm the Business Development Manager here," he began, the weight of responsibility evident in his voice. "I lead the sales team, handle client identification, and oversee our proposal preparations and bid submissions." As he spoke, I noted a subtle change in his demeanor, one that hinted at a keen sense of proprietorship and a dash of ego.

By contrast, Jim exuded a can-do attitude, combined with a genuine desire for improvement. “I manage the day-to-day activities of our employees who interact with our clients,” he shared, “and I manage the operational deliveries to our clients too. It’s my job to make sure the right workers are hired, the clients are satisfied with their products, and to handle the true cost, schedule, and performance of each of the contracts we are involved in.”

Susan went last. She sat up a little taller, her hands folded and resting on the edge of the table in front of her. “I am Susan, the Finance manager. I oversee the daily finances as well as all of the AR/AP and Contracting,” she said quickly and quietly.

After getting to know the team and their roles, I was curious about how they collaborated.

“Steve, when you come across challenges in your role, how do you and Liv work them out?” I was eager to understand the dynamics of their professional relationship, to see if it matched what Liv had previously conveyed.

Steve hesitated just a bit, “Usually, I just handle it with my team.”

Obviously, Steve leaned more towards an entrepreneurial approach, looking for opportunities and expanding the business. But was he truly building relationships with potential clients? Or just sending out proposals blindly?

"About your bids," I probed, "when you're preparing them, do you establish a relationship with the potential client first?"

His response was almost defensive, "We do our research."

"But do you have a relationship with the customer?" I pressed further.

The brief silence was telling. "No, we usually rely on our research."

I nodded, mentally noting areas of potential improvement.

I turned my attention to Jim. "Jim, when you run into problems, how do you solve them?"

"Uhh…first I try to understand the problem. If it is a minor one that can be fixed in-house, I will do that."

"...And if it is a bigger problem?" I asked.

"If I come across something I'm uncertain about, I bring it to Liv's attention immediately."

"How do you ensure that the people you hire are a fit for the roles you need? Do you have a metric to measure their capabilities with?"

He pondered for a moment before answering. "We ensure they meet the job description requirements. They also have to fit in with our company culture."

"But do you dive deep into their skills, matching them to specific job requirements?"

Another pause. "No. We primarily ensure they're a culture fit."

"You and I can speak further on this, Jim." I stated.

"I look forward to it," he answered. I could tell he honestly meant it.

It was becoming clear that processes needed to be established and improved. The company was profitable, but there were evident gaps in their operations.

Sue, we will let you jump in soon, but I need to make sure I understand the hand off between Operations and Business Development for my first step.

"You are doing commendable work," I began, choosing my words carefully, "but there's always room for refinement. Together, we can optimize your processes, ensuring growth and improving efficiency."

Taking a deep breath and sitting up straight, I glanced around the table, locking eyes with each one of them, ensuring I had their undivided attention.

"Okay. So, everybody," I began, striving to sound more encouraging, "thanks for your information." I paused momentarily, choosing my next words carefully. I wanted to communicate both authority and collaboration. "I think I can jump in at a couple of places here. There are things I believe we can tweak."

Steve leaned back in his chair, his eyes narrowing slightly, betraying the internal gears turning as he processed my words. Jim, more animated, tilted his head, acknowledging my point and appearing eager to know what came next.

"I definitely want to do a deeper dive with each one of you in your department," I continued, with emphasis on "each one". "We'll start working through those areas that we need to look at."

Susan, who had been silent for a while, scribbled something on her notepad, her eyebrows furrowing in concentration. I wondered what she was thinking.

"Let's take a break. Jim," I directed my gaze to him, "I'd like for us to spend some time together after lunch." I then shifted my attention to Steve, "And Steve, we'll meet up after that so I can understand your processes."

Jim nodded enthusiastically, seemingly excited about the opportunity to share and collaborate. Steve, on the other hand, simply responded with a curt nod, possibly processing the potential implications.

"And we'll go from there," I concluded, aiming to inject a note of positivity and forward momentum into the atmosphere.

Liv, always the mediator, smiled reassuringly, "It's an opportunity for growth for all of us. We appreciate your insights, Brian."

I nodded, grateful for her support, "Now we get to work together to optimize your processes, improve efficiency and grow this company to where you want it to be. I will also want to discuss how your relationships with each other and others outside the company work. I feel that relationships and relationship management are key to success across many of the processes and can help with some of the efficiencies. I'm excited for the progress ahead," I said as I gathered my notes and stood up. "Let's make it happen," I said with a determined smile.

We all got up and started making our way to the door, "Liv, would you like to grab some lunch and go over my initial thoughts?"

"Of course, there are usually food trucks in the parking lot. Want to go have a look?"

Operational Department Overview

The door to Jim's office swung open, revealing a space filled with well-organized piles of papers and multiple certificates of achievement on the walls. I entered the room, taking in the sight of Jim sitting behind his desk, looking poised yet expectant.

"Jim," I said as I shook hands with him again and then took a seat across from him. "I wanted to hear more about your managerial processes. Could you walk me through it?"

Jim took a deep breath and nodded. "Of course. How do I manage my team, you mean?"

"Exactly," I affirmed. "We've already touched on how you hire. Now, how do you get feedback to and from Steve's team when you see opportunities for growth? Do you pass warm leads over to them? How closely do you focus on the customer's needs and how do you cultivate those partnerships?"

"Well, I get weekly and biweekly reports from my team about the clients and the trends they are seeing in the company or questions that the company is asking. They also inform me about their deliverables. But when it comes to Steve and his team, I mostly focus on the customer's needs."

"And relationship management? How do you manage it on your level, and how does your on-site team handle it?" I probed.

Jim seemed momentarily taken aback, but he collected himself quickly. "I have regular check-ins with my clients, and I conduct a survey with them twice a year."

I raised an eyebrow. "But how often do you personally talk to the individual who is buying your services?"

"Well," Jim hesitated, "at least once a quarter or maybe twice a year." *Not good,* I thought to myself.

"What happens if managers change out? How long does it take you to know?" I pressed.

Jim looked a little self-conscious. "I usually find out and introduce myself during my next scheduled visit."

"So, if managers change, you don't immediately go to introduce yourself to them as one of their primary providers?" I asked.

"No," he said. "I just do it on my routine."

"That's a potential missed opportunity," I pointed out, leaning forward for emphasis. "We can address that in our communications plan. That is an area where you could build a stronger relationship with a client. If a manager changes, you have to introduce yourself as one of their main providers immediately. It's a chance to create a firm bond with the new manager, ensuring a smoother transition. Additionally, this is a good opportunity to gain an understanding of new tasks his boss has given him and upcoming potential changes that may have been directed."

Jim's face showed a mix of realization and reflection. "I hadn't thought of it that way."

I shifted in my chair, deciding to address another topic. "Do you and Liv discuss your personal and professional aspirations? Where do you envision yourself in five years?"

His eyes lit up with ambition. “In five years? I want to continue helping the company grow and leading multiple verticals as the COO.”

I nodded. “Have you outlined the education and skills, both personally and professionally, you’d need to reach that role?”

He hesitated. “Not really.”

“That’s something you need to look at,” I advised. “You and Liv need to talk about this. If that’s what you want, to take it to that level, you have to create a professional growth plan. These things don’t happen by accident. Set a plan and set milestones. Make sure both you and the company can be held accountable.”

Jim took a moment, absorbing the information. “That’s a great idea. I’ll definitely discuss this with Liv. It’s a good recommendation.”

I decided to wrap up, since Jim needed to prepare for his next meeting. “Is there anything else you’d like to cover?”

Jim shook his head, a hint of gratitude in his eyes. “You’ve given me a lot to ponder.”

“Okay then,” I said, packing up. “If anything comes up, you know how to get a hold of me. I’ll go back, capture my notes from this and be ready to talk to you about next steps in a few weeks when I come back.”

This couldn't have gone any better, I thought as I exited the room.

Business Development Department Overview

Steve's office felt different from Jim's space. While Jim's area exuded a sense of grounded methodical approach, Steve's environment was alive with activity, papers strewn about and various analytical tools flashing on computer screens. I poked my head in. Steve was standing up, writing something on a whiteboard. When I rapped lightly on the door he turned around.

"Brian," he greeted me. "Please, come in. Sit down." He gestured to the chair in front of his desk. As I sat, he settled himself into his chair behind it.

"Hello, Steve," I began, "I just wrapped up with Jim. We were talking about operational challenges. We need to come up with some processes so he can feed you better information on how to grow with the current customers. Have you thought about working with Jim on gathering data on current customers? What insights are you gleaning from your research and discussions with current partners?"

Steve leaned back and said, "Well, I use salesforce, business analysis tools and the like. We pull our insights from there and I don't currently have a process for Jim and I to talk about the current customers. We just catch that as part of normal operations meetings."

"Okay. So, you have the data you would need to start your conversation with new customers?"

"Yes, we do," he replied.

"How do you identify with a new customer you need to talk to?" I asked.

"We usually touch base with their sales or buying teams to know what they're purchasing and when they'll be requesting quotes. Then we follow their procedures," he explained.

"But do you ever actually engage them, talk to them, maybe have coffee?" I pressed.

Steve sighed, "Look, I'll be straight with you Brian." I could hear the first notes of annoyance in his voice. "We're swamped writing proposals and doing research. We barely have time for direct sales."

Raising an eyebrow, I replied, "So, what you're saying is you don't really have a relationship management model to make yourself closer or stickier to the customer."

Steve looked genuinely puzzled. He sounded slightly exasperated but he was doing his best to cover it up. "What do you mean by that?"

"Every sale has a methodology, Steve," I explained, ignoring his irritation. "You figure out who the three to five key people in the organization you want to talk to are. No matter what it is they are buying, there are going to be a very small number of people who are the catalyst for procurement and relationships. Maybe we can set up a process for you to move towards relationship management.[4] Doing it this way actually saves you time. If you're identifying these people and managing your relationship with them, you could be writing fewer proposals and winning more because you're a better customer and a better partner to your customer.

"That is not how we do business," he said.

"Even if the way you're doing business is wrong?" I asked.

"It just doesn't work like that here," he insisted.

"Hold on, Steve," I was starting to get a little frustrated. "All businesses work the same. It is about the people. Your buyers are *people.* It's not as if you're loading your proposals into some machine or AI bot and that's what's deciding yay or nay. And if they are using AI or machine learning or some type of technology tool to screen through the proposals for value, you need to understand how they use those tools. And that will only come through relationship management—having the right discussions with the right people."

"I guess that is something we can look at." His tone was unenthused. "It's just not the way we've done it in the past," he said reluctantly." I nodded. "Change is hard, but it's also

---

[4] See Chapter 6

necessary. If you don't know your customers, if you don't talk to them, then someone else will."

Steve's eyes were full of skepticism. "I guess I can look into it."

"It's usually the person who has spoken with the customer most that has the inside edge when they're evaluating proposals. Even if you have an amazing product, use all the buzz words and have a visually appealing proposal, the person with the best relationship generally gets the thumbs up when it comes to bids because that's who they trust.

"What do you do when you or your team runs into a problem?" I questioned.

"We don't run into problems," he proudly announced with a twitch of his head.

"No? How many failed bids did Liv say you had in the past year? Fifty? I have to assume that you ran into *some* problems along the way," I stated very matter-of-a-factly.

He didn't answer. I know what I had just said wounded his pride and embarrassed him. He looked down at the floor and cleared his throat.

"What is your plan to attract more clients?"

"To keep bidding."

"But that's not working. Do you not see that?"

Still more silence.

"So, what's the five-year plan then, Steve?

"We'll grow the company by three-hundred percent. The data analytics market is growing rapidly. We will be able to capture some of that market share."

"How?" I asked.

"Excuse me?" He questioned.

"How will you capture the market share? Please do not say you will keep bidding. What's the strategy? What metrics will you use?"

He didn't have an answer. I could feel some resentment in the undercurrent of the silence.

"If you have a vision that this business would develop within the next five years, why have you not yet written your plan for this vision?"

"We have been busy writing proposals," he said.

"You've just been throwing stuff at the wall and seeing what sticks. But almost nothing is sticking. Have none of your writers asked you why all the bids they've been writing have failed? Do you know why you're failing?" I asked.

"I just think if we keep doing our research and writing good proposals…" he trailed off.

"It's not working Steve. We need to figure out the relationship management between you, your writers, and your tech folks because if they are blindly writing you stuff that fits the market without asking you questions, it's no wonder you went as far as fifty bids without any success. We have got to look at why you are not being successful if we want things to change."

Steve was looking out of the window at that point, nodding his head but saying nothing.

I stood up and picked up my backpack. "I think this is a good start. We both have some things to think about. I know we will find the right solutions for you, your department and the company as long as we work together, listen to one another and are open to change." Steve looked down at the floor and then back at me. He didn't say anything, but acknowledged he had heard what I said by a short quick nod and a soft but begrudging grunt.

Charting A New Course

Liv met me in the hallway as I was coming out of Steve's office. "Let's talk and walk," I said.

As we walked through reception, I waved to Kerry, who waved back immediately. Her cheerful attitude really did make me smile. When we were clear of the office and as we went down the hall to the elevator I started talking.

"Liv, your team is not building relationships with your current customers. That is what is root causing most of your growth operational problems. As for your business development team, we need to put metrics in place because Steve does not have any. He is only doing basic research when you get a request for a quote or proposal, and we are writing those proposals based on that research. We don't really know how the people buying from you are evaluating your products."

"As for Jim," I continued, "his department needs to establish operational metrics for better customer interaction. You might not have fully realized the extent of your clients' potential spending on your products. I think you're leaving money on the table, there. There could be untapped markets in other departments within the companies you're working with that could benefit from your data analytics and business analysis products. To uncover these possibilities, you'll need to get closer to them and understand their needs. It'll also help you identify other companies in that niche. Then operations can give feedback to the BD team, and that will help shape the conversation with the new client."

"Our new potential client," she said quickly.

"We'll get there," I reassured her.

"You've given all of us a lot to think about, thank you." I could hear both relief and excitement in her voice. "So, how do we move forward?"

"The next step is to start working through your people, your process, and your operations."

We arrived at my silver Ford truck in a lighter mood.

"Nice car,"she smiled appreciatively.

"I am patriotic, ma'am. Always buy American."

I turned the radio on as I drove home that afternoon. All in all, it was a pretty good day. Everything worked out the way I had planned it, and I could see that the company would achieve its goal before we were done with the consultation. The only hiccup was Steve and his negative attitude, but I knew he would come around eventually.

CHAPTER FOUR

THE GOAL TRILOGY: SETTING, SHARING, AND SCRUTINIZING YOUR TARGETS

The early morning sun hit my eyes as I pulled into the parking lot two weeks later. I was looking forward to what the day would hold. What challenges and successes would we have today? I parked the truck, quickly checked my reflection in the rearview mirror, and made my way towards the building.

I felt a lively sense of anticipation as I entered and walked across the lobby to the elevator. When I got to the office I gave a nod to the receptionist. "Hello, Kerry. Nice to see you again."

"Back again so soon?" she asked with a grin.

"Yeah, round two," I replied.

"We're all excited for the changes we're going to be making," she smiled. "Liv's waiting for you in her office. Coffee? Water?" *She is so perky,* I thought. *Exactly the type of person you want as the first face people see coming through the door. A Director of First Impression as I say.*

"Coffee would be great, thank you. Black," I said.

"Coming right up! Why don't you go back there and I'll bring it to you." I could feel something different in the air as I walked down the hallway. It was lighter somehow. When I got to her office, Liv was behind her desk on the phone. She waved me inside. I took a seat on the couch, running my hand over the fabric as I did. It was soft, but durable. Kerry appeared with my coffee and I mouthed *Thank you* at her as she placed it on the table in front of me and cheerily slid out.

I looked over at Liv. Her face was *saying sorry about this,* as her upright finger was saying *just give me one minute.* Glancing around the room, I noticed a small bookcase with a stack of four or five books on top. I'm always curious about the titles people have in their office. *The E-Myth Revisited* held the place of honor atop the pile. Matthew Kelly's *Dream Manager* was right underneath. I saw Robert Kiyosaki's *Rich Dad, Poor Dad,* and Napoleon Hill's *Think and Grow Rich* in there as well. They all looked like they had been read several times. I was impressed; they are all great books that have helped me in my business.

"Sorry, I cleared my schedule before you got here but this was a last-minute situation," Olivia said as she took a seat in one of the chairs across from me.

"It's fine, Liv. You sounded excited when checking in with me for this appointment. Tell me why."

"Of course," she said. She had a glint in her eyes that had not been there during the other meetings we'd had. "It's amazing!"

"What is?" Her excitement was contagious.

"Everything! The company has not been the same since the last time you were here."

"Tell me about it."

"When you left that Friday, I spoke to everyone about the points you noticed. After that, they all sulked around throughout the day, especially Steve. He wouldn't even talk to me about it. He didn't do any more work that day. He just left the office for the weekend," an unhappy look took over her face momentarily.

"And Jim?" I asked.

She perked up. "Nothing could tear him away from his desk. He had his team get the files on the companies we currently support. They also told me that he practically interrogated each of them, asking several questions about how they saw themselves fitting in with the company. One of them was scared that she'd lose her job because Jim wasn't satisfied with the answers she gave."

I chuckled in amusement. It sounded to me like in his excitement to get started he might have gotten a little over zealous, but that is better than caving inward.

"Monday morning, Steve came to work, grabbed his records and started to make a ton of calls to the folks he knew at our current clients' companies," Liv continued. "I have no idea what he said, but a couple of our clients have been calling to schedule meetings to discuss their portfolios with us. He must have started to rekindle the original relationships he had with them."

She began talking so quickly, she was almost out of breath. "I was working on OnePenny's proposal when you came in," she continued. "They've been our clients since we opened shop but they had always resisted every time we proposed anything more than what was their status quo. Now they've sent *us* a proposal to review. I still have unopened emails from Monolith, Savia, and Lione. They are all customers who are engaging to understand more from Steve's call and how to discuss our data analytics service for their other departments. Steve carved that magic out of thin air."

"He just did what I told him to," I responded with a smile on my face.

"What is that?" she questioned.

"He renewed his relationships with the managers of those companies. That way it's much easier for him to 'open their eyes' as to how more departments in their companies could use your service as well," I said.

"You said we were leaving money on the table with our current clients. I didn't realize how much!" she expressed.

"I'm glad he worked on it and that you're so excited. I just want to caution you to keep in mind that this is the easy part," I reluctantly reminded her. "These were the original folks you guys started with. The relationships were already established, Steve just rekindled them. They're not the 50 failed proposal clients." Liv's smile faltered a little and she looked down. "Tell me about the changes in operations."

"Jim's been working like a man possessed. He's really inspiring his team, too. Look at that file on my desk there," she turned around and pointed at a thickish file. "That contains several suggestions about how we can improve our operations. I'm sure you noticed a change just walking in here. This place has not been this lively for a long time. If it wasn't for the growth I'm really aiming for, I could almost say they can now handle things just fine without me watching their every move. Steve has never been this serious since he was in the Army."

"Now something's driving him," I stated.

"What's that?" she asked.

"The desire to stick it to me. He wants to show me I made a mistake by underestimating him." I laughed. I was starting to think I might have.

Leading with Intent: Strategizing with Clarity and Purpose

"What are we talking about today then, Brian?" she asked, her voice crisp. "Let's get into it."

I took another sip of coffee. "Okay, so far we've talked to your team, some. We diagnosed a few problems and discussed some solutions. The next phase for us involves setting clear goals for you, mapping out your strategic plan, and determining how your campaign looks."

Her eyebrows drew together in confusion. "Campaign? Campaign for what?"

I leaned forward, eager to clarify. "By campaign I mean your plan for how you intend to shape the way your leaders follow you. Where would you like them to focus? Do you have a targeted customer list? We want to make sure your direct reports understand your vision and how they fit into it. We'll lay out a roadmap for the company and they've got to have buy-in because they will have to present, coach and mentor it to their subordinates."

"Okay," Liv murmured, tapping a finger against her chin thoughtfully. "So how do we put together this roadmap?"

"You need to create growth goals and plans for one, two and three year periods. We will have a strategic planning session where we set goals[5]. Then we break the goals up and spread

---

[5] Chapter 7

them across the team so that the responsibility doesn't lie heavily on a single department."

"Yeah," Liv leaned back in her chair, pondering. "That'll put a lot of stress on every department. We don't want to overtax any particular one. Expanding our workforce and the number of projects we are handling has to be done in a balanced way," she was almost muttering to herself.

I nodded in agreement. "You've got it. We'll set a strategy for achievements[6] in each department. Then based on whether it's a one-year, two-year, or three-year plan, we decide what the accomplishments should be on the way to meeting those goals."

"But how do we decide the goals?"

I took another sip of coffee to give myself a moment to collect my thoughts. "The process is a two-way street. We'll be asking for a lot of feedback from your subordinates, and their subordinates," I explained. "They're the ones in the trenches, actually experiencing everything. We want to know what they think could go wrong and what they think could go right. Then when we're setting our goals and determining our metrics we don't set outlandish objectives that can't be achieved."

"That would be seriously demoralizing for the team," Liv said, tilting her head as she processed. "So, we are back to the goals you were talking about a few weeks ago?"

---

[6] Chapter 7

I grinned, glad she remembered."Yes, SMART Goals. But while we set realistic goals, we also want to set a stretch goal if we want to push ourselves a little bit. This is where the relationship between you and your direct reports and their direct reports is key. You come up with these goals together. We may want to stretch but we don't want to be setting a goal that they don't think we can reach."

"So how do we balance ambition and reality?"

I glanced at the wall behind her, filled with framed achievements of the company. My eyes fell on a picture of her and Steve when they were serving together. It made me smile.

"Think of it like a military strategy. Let's say they decide they want to do a campaign in Europe. The generals set a broad objective. The detailed planning—the operations—are left to the subordinates. They determine how to achieve the broader objective by breaking the overall goal into accomplishments that can be measured toward success as incremental steps. Similarly, you'll set the overarching strategy for the company, your directors will determine what the campaign will look like, and your managers will tackle the nitty gritty details, ensuring accountability."

I paused for a moment, letting the analogy sink in. Liv's posture was tense, eyes slightly narrowed, and she was looking slightly to the side, absorbing the information. She was sitting all the way back in her chair, her fingers entwined in her lap. Her brow furrowed, her lips pressed into a thin line. I could tell she was doing a lot of processing. "Do you have any questions?"

She took a deep breath and exhaled slowly, clearly trying to organize her thoughts. "Yeah. You've used the words 'vision,' 'goal' and 'achievement.' I'm a little confused about the difference."

A small smile crept onto my face. "Great point. It's pretty easy, actually. Your vision is your big picture, right? But your goals are the steps that lead to that final big picture. Right behind that are accomplishments."

She tilted her head slightly, her eyes searching mine for clarity. "And the accomplishments are…?"

"The steps you take to achieve your goals," I explained, hoping the layers were becoming more transparent for her.

"Have you ever heard of the DOD's Iron Man suit project?" I asked, watching her eyes light up in recognition. "That's a prime example of setting visionary goals. They said, 'Okay, we want to make this soldier that could function non-stop for 24 hours a day, leap tall buildings, cross the ocean, run at light speed and not have a heart attack, pass out or kill himself."

Liv leaned in, her interest piqued. "I remember that. It seemed like something straight out of a sci-fi movie."

I nodded. "Exactly. But to do that, they had to dissect each one of those attributes into achievable components. They studied all aspects—technology, manufacturing, and delivery. The Iron Man suit was more than just armor; it was about enhancing every single vertical that contributed to its functionality. It meant we had to create stronger, faster, lighter, better batteries, for example."

"Ohhhhhh…." her eyes opened wide and her mouth was the shape of an *O*. I laughed. She was getting it.

"We needed body armor that was much lighter. We needed to give it some type of augmented strength in its arms and legs, so that it could lift more and run faster. So, we broke the idea for the suit down into its basic elements."

"So you could work on each separately."

"Yes, then break it down further. Take the helmet—its display had to react the way real eyes react and have a breathing apparatus to help the soldier breathe underwater."

"That is so cool!"

"I know! But the Iron Man suit wasn't what the task was really about. It was about advancing technology. We had to take a look at where we were with current technology and then figure out how we could put our foot on the throttle, push the boundaries in all of these areas and see where we could make a breakthrough."

"So," she leaned forward, "if I'm understanding this correctly, advancing technology was the vision. The Iron Man suit was the goal, and lighter armor, augmented strength, better batteries, running across water, leaping buildings—all those things were the accomplishments."

"That's it. And then how you do it is your strategy." She settled back into the chair, satisfied. I went on, "And when we get going, you'll see how successes, adaptations, achievements and goals spill into other departments."

"What do you mean?" she asked, looking for clarification.

"It's like the Star Wars program under Reagan. He thought the doctrine of Mutually Assured Destruction was crazy—that's how it got the name MAD. Anyway, he set a goal for the US to render nuclear attacks inefficient. Ultimately the goal was to make a massive system that could shoot down everything that flew into U.S. airspace. It was the DoD's project. They worked on missiles, radars, tracking, explosives and the like. Each one of those areas improved and therefore affected things like the way the FAA tracks aircraft because it advanced radar technology. That's just one example."

"Okay, that's really interesting…but how does that come into play here?"

"Business development will work to improve their functions, which will create better proposals. Those proposals lead to better wins for Operations to implement. Now they can be more efficient because a project comes in better scoped and more accurate. That will translate into being able to refine engineering time, IT support, and other pieces can be refined. Now there are costs that you would have had for a very loose proposal that you now don't have.

Liv's eyes lit up with every layer of my answer. When I was finished, she stared at me thinking about all of the possibilities.

Setting Strategic Goals

I let that sit for a few moments. Then we went right back into it. "Ready to start setting some goals?"

She clapped her hands in front of her loudly. "Yes!" she almost shouted.

"Great." I opened my backpack and rifled through it. "Here's a worksheet for us to fill out. This will help us get started." I said, as I handed the form to Liv.

<table>
<tr><th colspan="3">The Vision Overview</th></tr>
<tr><td>CORE VALUES</td><td>1.
2.
3.
4.
5.</td><td>3-YEAR PICTURE</td></tr>
<tr><td>CORE FOCUS</td><td>Purpose/Cause/Passion:

Our Niche:</td><td rowspan="3">Future Date:
Revenue:
Profit:
Measurables:
What Does It Look Like?
•
•
•
•
•
•
•
•
•
•</td></tr>
<tr><td>5-YEAR TARGET</td><td></td></tr>
<tr><td>MARKETING STRATEGY</td><td>Target Market/The List:

3 Unique's 1.
2.
3.
Proven Process

Guarantee:</td></tr>
</table>

"Now, the Core Values and Core Focus I'm going to leave to you to fill out on your own time. We are looking at the *Five-year Target* and *Marketing Strategy* and *Three Year Picture* pieces."

She was looking the worksheet over and nodding her head as I spoke.

"So what's the five-year target?" I asked her.

"At least one-hundred percent growth, national expansion and at least one international contract," she said succinctly, not even looking up, as she wrote it down.

"Excellent. Okay, down in *Marketing Strategy,* for now we are just going to take a look at the *Target Market*. Who do you want to be doing business with?"

"Both commercial businesses and governmental departments."

"Where?"

"National and international."

"Great. The next thing we ask is how would a normal business of your size grow? So, if you want to double in three to five years, when we break that down, that is a fifteen to twenty percent growth per year. But, like we were saying, we don't want to give that all to one department, so we will need to figure out what percentage each department gets. We'll get into the nitty gritty of that later in our discussions.[7]"

"I'm looking forward to that one," she smiled.

So that means under *Three Year Picture* we are looking for revenue to be $9 million and our profits around eight to ten percent" I stopped and looked at my watch. "Let's take a break and reconvene in twenty minutes in the conference room with Jim, Susan and Steve."

"What about the rest of the sheet?" she asked, bewildered.

---

[7] See Chapter 6

"Don't worry," I reassured her, laughing, "we'll get there. And then we also need to look at your processes,[8] particularly how you're doing your analytics and business intelligence; we want to make sure that you're doing each task in the most efficient way you can, because wasted man-power and wasted money count against you when you're a small business trying to grow." *She looks a little like a kid in a candy-store,* I thought, as we got up and walked out of her office.

Articulating and Aligning our Team

Twenty minutes and one latte later, we were in the conference room with Susan and Jim when Steve came strutting through the door. He came over to me with a smirk on his face. "Good morning, Brian. Great to see you," he greeted me in a voice that was a bit ironically over-pleased, as he extended his hand to give me a power-handshake. *That was quite an entrance,* I thought, wholly amused. *Is he going to jump up on the table and start beating his chest?*

"I assume Liv told you about all our progress?" he gloated, as we were all sitting down.

"She did indeed," I answered with a smile. "Good work."

Once everyone was seated, I addressed the room.

---

[8] See Chapter 6

“Thank you for coming. It’s good to see all of you again.” Jim was still smiling widely, whereas Steve just looked smug.

“Liv and I have been talking about goals today, and we wanted to bring you guys in.”

“So let’s talk about communication,” I began. “And that starts with *who* you will be communicating with.”

“There’s an approach I’ve already discussed with Liv a few weeks ago. One up, two down. That is, your direct report and those who report directly to you.”

“So it’s about consistent information flow?” Jim piped up, “Top to bottom?”

“Yes, Jim. But it’s not just top-down; feedback should be encouraged from the ground up as well.”

Steve raised an eyebrow. “Like the whole suggestion box thing?”

“That’s right.”

“So, can they offer feedback? Like, if they see something being promised that they can’t deliver?” Jim asked quickly. Steve turned his head to look at Jim; his body stiffened slightly, and his lips compressed into a line. Jim avoided looking at Steve. I saw Liv’s eyes ticking back and forth between the two of them a couple of times, with a slightly concerned look on her face. *There is something there,* I thought, but I wanted to stay on point, so I continued.

“That is something we definitely would want to know about. We want to hear about *any* flaw the employees come up against and any suggestions for enhancements. They should be empowered to liaise with the business development team and with finance to make company improvements. You could even offer an incentive for ideas that will save the company money.”

Steve, unable to hide his irritation at Jim’s question completely, quipped, “Ah, yes, press the lever, you get an award approach.”

I met Steve’s challenging gaze relaxed, with the hint of a smile on my face. “It’s not just about the rewards, Steve. It’s about creating a space where employees feel their voice matters.”

“So incentives can ensure that the dialogue between levels remains open.” Liv jumped in quickly. “Which ensures the flow of information can go both ways throughout the organization. To do that, we want the employees to know that their feedback is desired so they are comfortable coming to us, right?”

“Precisely, Liv,” I said. “Now this type of communication is something we want to be ubiquitous throughout the company, but let’s turn our attention really quickly to how we communicate goals, specifically.”

Both Jim and Liv leaned forward. Steve sat back in his chair, tapping his lips with a pen and shifting his legs so that the seat of his chair twisted from one side to the other, back and forth.

"Since the owner decides on the important skills, Liv," I said, "you have to really grasp what you're asking of your team. And equally crucial, understand how you intend to hold them accountable."

Liv nodded thoughtfully, a slight crease forming on her forehead. "So, I need to communicate effectively and set clear expectations."

"Exactly," I confirmed. "And it's the same for the directors." I motioned to Steve and Jim. "They should know the strategic direction you're setting, ensuring their initiatives align with it. This way, everyone's efforts mesh perfectly."

"So, everyone's 'rowing' in the same direction?" Steve asked. "Instead of being up a creek without a paddle."

"Yup," I laughed. Steve's smirk was back. But I wanted to emphasize the significance of alignment, so I continued, "Everyone should be clear on their role. Every employee is in harmony with your vision. When assigning a task to a manager it's crucial to validate the information with the layer below him. This way, you ensure that the director has cascaded the information correctly. Similarly, the managers should confirm that the team leads have disseminated the details accurately to the workers. It's a loop of constant feedback and realignment to your core vision."

Everyone sat back in their seats and took a moment to process. Liv and Jim jotted down notes. When he finished Jim looked up at me and asked, "So, this continuous check and balance is to guarantee that everyone's in sync with the broader objective?"

I nodded, "Exactly. This methodology allows us to pinpoint precisely what skills you require and in which department. We can then match these with your current capabilities. If there's a mismatch, either in terms of employee skill set or departmental ability, it's an area of concern. Such gaps could hinder you from realizing your goals."

Steve frowned, thoughtful. "So you're suggesting that we fire any person who isn't fulfilling their role or who isn't aligning with the strategy?"

"Yes, Steve," I replied. "But it's not about eliminating roles or employees hastily. It's about understanding where the gaps are and working towards filling them. We'll delve deeper into this when we discuss our organizational chart."[9]

Liv interjected, her analytical mind ever at work, "But how do we distinguish between a process issue and a personnel issue?"

"Good question, Liv," I commended. "With the constant evolution in tech, including software analysis and business intelligence, training becomes imperative. Sometimes, it's not the person, but the process that's flawed."

---

[9] See Chapter 5

Steve looked at me, "But surely, there must be instances where an employee can't adapt, even with training."

"You're spot on," I agreed. "In such cases, your approach still isn't immediate termination. Maybe they need a different training method. But if they still can't keep pace, you need to evaluate their fit within your goals and potentially redirect them to roles that better suit their strengths."

Liv's expression was one of concern. "How do we address employees who might not fit into the evolved strategy without demoralizing them?"

"You treat them with empathy," I stressed. "You don't just tell them 'It's not working out.' You engage in a dialogue, exploring alternate roles within the company that might be a better fit. However, if it's evident they can't align with your goals, you need to have a transition plan."

Jim leaned forward, intrigued, "Transition plan?"

"Yes," I affirmed, "You assist them in potentially finding a new role, offer retraining opportunities, or help them transition to their next chapter. You want them to depart as apostles of the company, not adversaries."

Liv nodded in understanding, "And in terms of realignment, how do we handle it?"

"That's where cross-training comes in," I explained. "Say an employee in the proposal department might be better suited for inside sales. You can't just switch them. You need to train them in the skills they need to ensure they seamlessly align with the set goals."

"So how do we set those goals?"

"Carefully," I joked. There was a little light laughter. I smiled, "But seriously, we do have to be careful. We'll set ambitious goals for 12, 24, and even 36 months. But you can't just blindly set these goals and hope the path takes us there. It's a climb, a step-by-step journey. And in that journey, the first 90 days, the first six months, they're pivotal. That's where your momentum begins."

Jim nodded eagerly, absorbing every word. "So, we need short-term milestones to guide us?"

"Exactly," I replied, smiling at his enthusiasm. "But here's where it gets intricate. Each department, each team, has its milestones. The challenge? Ensuring they align with your overarching vision."

My gaze then settled on Liv, "Liv, you've said that your vision is to be international, and your goal is to double your revenue in three to five years. So let's say that on the way there, you've set a benchmark. Let's say you want to get the BD operating at eighty percent efficiency in the next two years."

Liv nodded, "Sounds good to me."

Steve looked at her with a little attitude.

"But here's the thing," I continued, "If we set Steve's milestones to get there, and he's working with his team on these, the real question is: do they make sense within your broader framework? Have you considered the ripple effects?"

Steve, the critic, raised an eyebrow. "Ripple effects?"

"Yes," I leaned forward, addressing the entire group, "the second, third order effects. Say Steve tasks his department with this 80 percent target. Are you, as a company, prepared to implement the changes required to support this? Is the operations department prepared for that kind of influx of business?"

Steve looked contemplative but remained silent.

"It's not just about numbers," I pressed on, hoping to bring Steve into the fold of understanding. "What metrics will the business development team use? How will they bid? Manage their clients? How will those things affect the other areas of the company? Even your internal processes need scrutiny. The team will need to refine their approach, focusing not just on growth, but on sustainable, meaningful growth." I looked around at the people in the room and saw that I might have just confused them more by throwing all those things out at once.

"So first, there's the cost of your decisions. Let me use an analogy," I began. "Consider the push for electric cars on a national scale. It's an idea most people know about." I saw nods of agreement, even from Steve.

I pressed on, "The country wants all cars to be electric by 2036. Well, that's great. Everybody buys an electric car. What do we do with battery recycling? What does this mean for power consumption?"

Jim, the operations manager, leaned in, his curiosity evident, "So, you're saying our milestones need to consider the larger ecosystem?"

"Precisely," I said, with a nod. "Every decision has a cause and effect."[10]

Steve interjected, a hint of sarcasm in his voice, "So, are you suggesting we're like a country switching to electric cars without enough charging stations?"

I met his gaze, not backing down, "Yes, Steve. That's a perfect illustration. Imagine everyone suddenly buys an electric car. But where's the advancement in battery technology? Or the infrastructure to support these cars? Who's responsible for putting the infrastructure in place? Is it the county? The state? The nation?"

"So, in the company as we're moving goals around and setting parameters, we need to be thinking about every reaction," Liv said. "Therefore, before we can start planning

---

[10] Chapter 8

the changes we're going to do with BD, we have to ask *How will those changes affect BD? And how will they affect the other departments?*"

"Milestones, like charging stations, aren't just stepping stones; they're foundational. They power the journey ahead, and without them, we risk stalling before we even get started."

I continued, "Consider this. If you refine the proposal process in BD, streamlining it so you bid less but win more, what ripple effects might you see within the department? Perhaps it might necessitate more travel. Are you ready for your teams to be in front of these clients more frequently? To attend tech shows and understand cutting-edge technologies in your industry?"

Susan piped up, "S0 refining our process would mean being on the ground more, learning, networking, and understanding client needs better. We'd be spending more on travel and training."

I turned and looked at her. I had almost forgotten she was in the room. "Possibly, Susan. And that's the essence of cause and effect. Is the decision going to cost you more? Take the inline hot water heater. Everyone's keen on making the switch; shifting from natural gas to on demand water heaters. Problem is that you may have saved on your monthly water bill but if you're located in Florida, like we are, where backup generators are essential, the inline heater demands a larger and much more expensive generator. So as we look at options and plans, we have to think about the actions, reactions and costs related to the total cost of a lifecycle." They were all nodding their heads. That was a good sign.

I continued, "The essence of what we're trying to do here is to break down your goals in a way that resonates with every team member. Steve, you'll be setting clear targets for your team, ensuring that each one of them feels a sense of ownership."

Steve adjusted in his seat, nodding. "Right. I need to cascade my growth goal down to my team. Each of them will take on a segment of that responsibility."

"There's another issue we can't ignore: the bypass problem. Often, when a system, be it the acquisition system or even something like the country's immigration system, becomes problematic, the typical reaction is to create a workaround. Instead of solving the root issue, we erect new structures to bypass it."

Steve raised an eyebrow, "Like in the Department of Defense?"

"Exactly," I replied. "The DoD 5000 system, for instance, requires a revamp. But to do that, you're essentially looking at overhauling the entire federal acquisition process, followed by its defense counterpart. The enormity of the task often leads to circumvention rather than genuine solutions."

Jim sighed, "Not efficient."

"No," I agreed. "Often these workarounds aren't the most effective way forward, but they're what we resort to, to get out of doing the more comprehensive, more difficult, more expensive and more controversial work that, despite all those things, still needs to be done."

Steve smirked, "Only the government could afford such inefficiencies." There was a little light laughter.

"All right everyone," I said, looking at my watch. "This has been a lot. We still have a few more things to talk about but I think it's a good time for a break. Stretch your legs, let things kind of marinate. We'll come back in 20 minutes. Is that good?" There were some enthusiastic nods. We all got up, gathered ourselves and walked out of the room.

Metrics for Measuring Success

We all filed back into the conference room at the end of the break. I could tell just about everyone was feeling a bit overloaded and it was tiring them. Except for Jim. Somehow he was still at full power. But, majority rules and I decided to go through the last two topics I wanted to talk about quickly.

"Okay everyone," I addressed them all once everyone was seated. "I know we may be waning a little here. There are a few more things I want to go over and then we'll wrap up." Everybody just nodded their heads in agreement.

"I want to jump into measuring goals because we need to get it right for the whole team. I know some of you probably don't like to do evaluations because everybody wants a trophy these days. But we've got to be honest with everybody, so we can build real goals, build real measurables, so we can hold each other accountable." I looked around the room. I had everyone's attention.

"Accountability goes both ways. Your subordinates should be able to hold you accountable because there should be a dialogue on what you should be doing as a manager."

"Okay," said Jim. "That's actually really great. So how are we doing this?"

"I need to know from you guys how often you do your evaluations? Is this a monthly thing? Is this a quarterly thing?" They all just looked at each other like kids who knew the jig was up and were looking around to see who would 'fess up first.

Liv cleared her throat, "We do them yearly."

"Well, good thing I'm here, then. I'm going to recommend that we do this no less than quarterly. That kind of ties to your finances. It's kind of like when you go to the doctor and you get your blood tested. If you're between the top and the bottom number, the doctor doesn't care, but if you're outside the lines, we need to talk about it."

"Once we establish a goal, we want to make sure we have the capability, the money, the resources and everything for the goal so we can achieve it. A great example is the department of education. They are notorious for making a new policy and throwing it down to the 50 states to capture data, implement policy with no funding stream attached and the states don't even know it's coming. And then they have to figure it out in their budget—how many people they have to hire and what they have to do to be compliant."

"So if we tell someone to do something, we better make sure they have the tools to do it," Jim said.

"Yes, but it's not only tools," I continued. "It's purpose. We've got to know why we're collecting the data. If it's not helping us make decisions then it's pointless."

Liv leaned in, "So, we only gather data that helps move us forward. That makes sense."

If these reports are already in place, consider incorporating tables outlining the progress of your goals into these regular reports. This will ensure that you're continuously monitoring your progress. Remember, there's no one-size-fits-all approach to goal measurement; it should align with the structure of your company. You need to examine how you collect data, the frequency of data collection, and how you utilize that data."

"So, what is it we should be measuring?" Jim asked.

"The data for goal measurement could include stuff like sales projections, how many customers you're keeping, how much work your employees are getting done, how much of the market you're owning, or any other numbers that show your progress." I explained. "You need to collect the relevant information and then make a decision based on the results. Just as a doctor wouldn't ignore a problematic blood test, you can't ignore your goal data. If something's amiss, you might need to tweak the company's processes or get rid of an unnecessary data point."

"Of course another way to address bad information is keeping unnecessary or redundant policies."

"Can you give us an example of what redundant policies are?" asked Liv.

Policy Pruning

"Redundant policies refer to processes and procedures that have become obsolete or unnecessary but are still in effect. These policies often lead to extra bureaucracy and staffing, causing inefficiencies in the company's operations. It's like when new companies start with a handful of procedures, but over time, these procedures multiply, many of which become outdated or irrelevant. Your company is still young, but there might already be policies that are outdated and redundant.

"I worked for a General Officer who took charge of the organization and announced that all policies are hereby rescinded and in all cases use your best judgment. His move instantly created chaos, with a line forming outside the Chief of Staff's office in just half an hour. The Chief of Staff had to clarify that although the General Officer had scrapped the existing policies, any new policy needed to go through a proper review process. If the company policy manual has become so bulky that employees are ditching it as soon as they get it, there's a problem. It's worth the effort to regularly review and update these policies to ensure they're still relevant to your operations."

"We use all our policies," Steve snapped.

"There will still be policies you don't use anymore, or the process may have changed," I said, standing my ground. "You should check your company's policies to filter these out or update them."

"That can be done weekly from now on," Jim suggested.

"Weekly is too much," I answered. "A monthly or quarterly review will work just fine."

I was silently grateful that Liv was smart enough to promote this man to manager.

"Alright, folks, that's a wrap for today's meeting," I announced. Steve promptly stood up and excused himself. Jim lingered briefly for a handshake before bidding us farewell and exiting the conference room. Liv was the last one left. "I'll walk you to your truck," she said smiling.

When we were out of the office I turned to her and said, "Liv, I trust you've noted everything we've talked about. I know you'll put it into action; your commitment is clear."

"Thank you again, Brian," she said sincerely.

"It's no problem. I'm just doing my job. Let's plan to meet again next week. Before that, could you prepare a list outlining your vision, goals, and the strategy for achieving them? When do you think you'll have that ready?" I asked."Sunday," she responded.

"Sunday it is. I'll be here again next Friday at the same time. Can you arrange for a whiteboard to be in your office for then?" I asked.

"Yes we have one here," she replied.

I have a lot of things to get organized before next week as we move to the next steps, I thought as I climbed into my truck.

CHAPTER FIVE

ORGANIZATIONAL STRUCTURE AND THE PATH TO COHESION: RESOLVING ROLES AND RIFTS

I walked into the meeting I had scheduled with Liv the following week with a heavy heart. I'd received a call from a business acquaintance of his company, Stylux. had finally shut down. I had met Dan, the founder and owner of Stylux, a year before. Although he knew next to nothing about business, he was a good man who treated everyone around him with respect. Unfortunately, his business was too far gone before he sought help.

Liv could see there was something amiss as soon as I walked in. "You seem distracted, Brian. Is everything all right?" I sighed and put my bag down. I told her about the unfortunate circumstances that had me feeling so glum.

"Could you have done something to help them?" she asked when I finished.

"I'm good at my job but sometimes a company just passes a point of no return and nothing can really be done to save it. It happens when a business owner ignores symptoms, even small ones, for too long. It's so sad and unnecessary for small businesses to fail when the owner has given it their all."

Liv commiserated, "So many people see asking for help as a weakness. They think they should be able to figure out everything on their own. But the fact is that asking for help is a sign of strength."

I sighed, "I just wish Dan had reached out sooner."

Understanding Business Beyond the Books

"So what happened with Stylux?" Liv asked. "Did they not have the money to scale because they overextended themselves or did they grow too fast? Did they hire the wrong people? Or didn't they have a proper strategy?" Liv asked with a note of concern in her voice. She did not want her company to suffer the same fate. Still, I was impressed; it was clear she had been listening as we discussed these issues over the previous weeks.

"In my opinion, business schools have failed a lot of people and business owners. The schools try to cookie-cut their education, but they forget to consider application and the people. Remember the people and the relationships they have with one another are the crux of a company. Any business owner worth their salt will tell you that human resources are the hardest resource to manage." I have even heard from a friend of mine Jeff, when asked in a business when do employee problems begin? He answered, "As soon as you hire the first one."

Liv gave a sad smile as I continued, "This is the reason owners such as yourself see there is something missing and you call me. This shows you are ready to look a little deeper under the hood to see what you might be overlooking."

"Yeah, better to know than not to," Liv agreed.

"Yes. And when I come in, I immediately start looking at the company and their relationship management; whether it's with employees, investors, or potential clients. Relationship management is the path to growth. So, you need to make sure your strategy and your business plan is something you can execute. I have seen too many business plans that have a lot of data and facts, but they do not have the operational wherewithal or the experience to scale them. When you plan your strategy, it should also identify the risks and the opportunities for failure. You need to put some thought into how you want your business to be built. Also know how you want to implement and with who to start the process."

Strategic Foundations: The Twin Pillars of Production and Scaling

"Let's talk about the two fundamental aspects of your strategy," I continued. "First and foremost, you need to understand the significance of your strategy and how it revolves around the relationships you build for success. Once you've got the strategy aspect figured out, you can delve into the manpower necessary to scale your delivery. Essentially, there are two critical parts to your strategy: production and scaling.

"The production aspect involves assessing whether you have the right people, processes, and equipment in place. On the other hand, the scaling part entails identifying who your target audience is going to be.

"The real key here is to focus on the details. It's not just about planning to sell your products but also understanding who your target market is. You can't be trying to sell ice to Eskimos, as the old adage goes. It's a waste of time and resources to pitch your product to those who don't need it or can't afford it. If your strategy doesn't outline a clear path to achieve your goals, it might be time to consider a revision."

"The devil is in the details," Liv said.

"It certainly is. Today, we will only be able to talk about the first part of your strategy, which is..." I opened the palm of my hand to her to show her that the question was meant for her.

"Building a company that makes what I want to sell," she said.

"Yes! Do you have the right people, processes, and equipment to build your business? Even more important is having the right people in the right position. So, it's really important for your strategy to create an organizational chart that includes all the different roles and functions your company needs to keep things running smoothly."

Mapping the Company: The Intricacies of the Organizational Chart

"Are we finally going to talk about the organizational chart?" Liv asked.

"Today's the day! The organizational chart details all the positions and departments in your company. It's like a pyramid—it starts from the very bottom of the company and goes all the way to the person on top. After you know how you plan to run the company, then you can figure out the people you need. Look at a Ford dealership, for example. If I want to run one, I'd need a salesman, a services department, a parts section and mechanics. All these functions will have to be present in my organizational chart. It's up to me to decide on the management structure. Who will answer to whom? How will information flow up and down that structure? Who will be responsible for what? It is the same for your business."

I handed her an example organizational chart to show her what one is supposed to look like."Let me walk you through the process of building an organizational chart. My approach is to draw the chart from the bottom up and then back down to ensure that no position is overlooked. You wouldn't want to finish your chart and then realize there's no role for a Financial Manager. After all, your money won't manage itself, will it? How else will you keep the IRS off your back? Every role in your business is crucial and deserves a place on your chart."

"Even the receptionist?" Liv asked.

"Yes. They are your company's introduction; the first face your clients or investors will see. Some have even called them the 'Director of First Impressions'. Of course they should be in your chart. It does not matter how inconsequential you think their role in your strategy is, as long as you need them to make your products or scale the business, they need a place in your chart.

"After you have found a place for every role you need, you can then write out the job descriptions for these roles. The job descriptions will tell you why you need each position within your strategy and the type of people you need in it. If your strategy requires a department of operations, for instance, your job description should explain that you need them to make the product and run the day-to-day activities of the company. Your chart will further highlight how you want the people in that department to be skilled technicians or proper negotiators. It all depends on what you want and the strategy you are building, as long as you keep the bare minimum of organizational chart building in mind."

"What is the bare minimum?"

"Every role should be listed. I once met a company that hired people to write out their organizational charts for them. Don't waste money like that. You and your key team should be able to do this. An outside person doesn't know all the functions and how they relate unless they really spend time with your team. They also don't account for companies being different and needing different organizational charts. If your business does not do government contracts, for example, you might not need a Contracts Department within your chart. A company like yours does not need a Security Department, at least not yet, but a retail store that doesn't have a Security Department, no matter how small, is not yet serious with its business. As long as you figure out your strategy first, your organizational chart will write itself. You will have a map overview from the strategy which identifies the direction you would like to go. Now let's show you how to fill out departments and build a successful company.

"There are basic departments that every company needs to fill, no matter what product you are selling. Without them, you cannot properly function. Of course, this does not mean you have to hire a person or an entire team for these departments. The responsibilities of the departments could be merged but you will need to communicate that in your organizational chart," I explained.

"What are the departments?"

"Note not all organizations are the same," I said, "so we have to build the chart based on what your company needs are."

I went on to explain to her that when I build a company, I create the departments on different levels. "OBIDA Global has three departments, so we will do a first level chart for each department: Operations, Business Development and Finance."

Operations Department (Operations Manager)

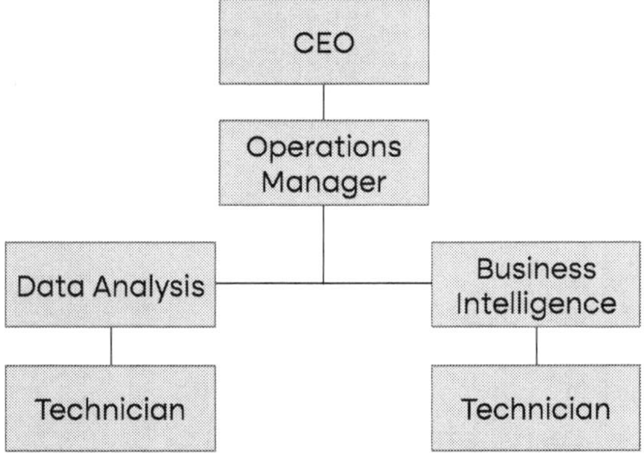

Fig. The Operations Department

Business Development Department (Business Development Manager)

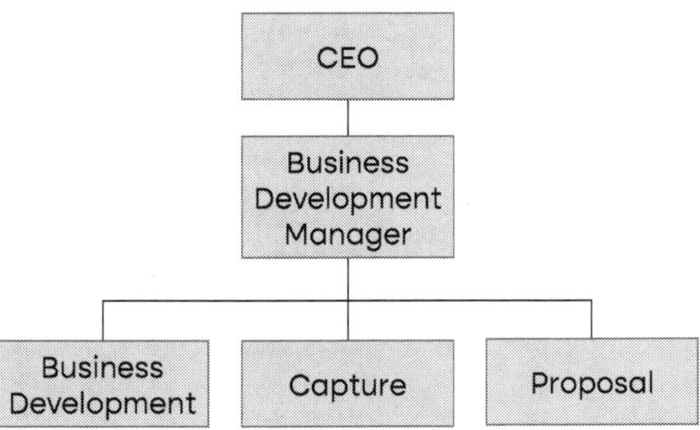

Fig. The Business Development Department

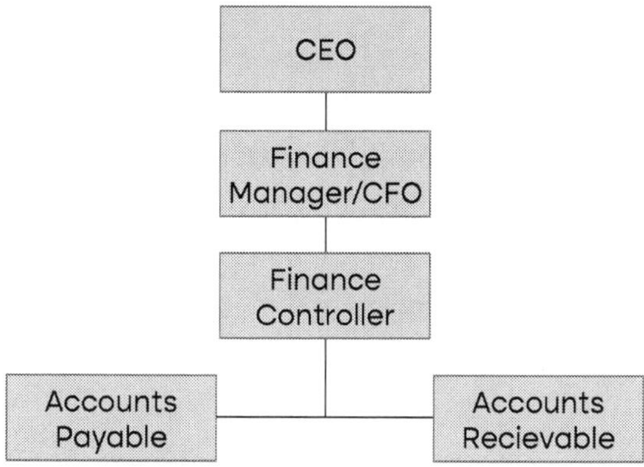

Fig. The Finance Department

The Core of Business Finance Management

"You'd be shocked to discover how many companies in the US don't hire anyone for the Procurement, Accounts Receivable (AR) and the Accounts Payable (AP) roles. They prefer to hire only a bookkeeper. In the end, it's the same as shooting yourself in the foot because there are so many things only a professional Finance Officer can advise you on.

"Many business owners select banks without considering the specific needs of their business. Having a Finance Officer would ensure a more strategic approach, such as evaluating multiple banks to find the most suitable one. Each bank offers different programs tailored to various business types and sizes. For instance, Bank A might have specific requirements, like a minimum revenue threshold, while a smaller bank might provide more favorable terms.

A Finance Officer can navigate these intricacies and offer valuable insights."

"Those three roles you said the finance department does, one person can do all that?" Liv asked.

"Yes but at some point when the company has grown, you have to divide the roles. One person can be in charge of AP/AR while another procures, and the other person controls the finances."

"How do the roles differ?"

"The AP/AR person will be in charge of your accounts payable and your accounts receivable. Your AP is the money you owe to your suppliers or anyone outside your business. They also check to make sure that what you order is what you get. AR is the money you're owed. Their role is to make sure every invoice in the business is accurate. It is a system of checks and balances. Now you see why these are roles you need to fill as fast as you can."

"What about the Controller?"

"They are the keepers of the funds. Their role is to know how much money the company should be getting and how much is leaving the company so that they don't overspend the treasury. In other words, they manage your cash flow. Your AP person pays the bills, but someone will need to check and see if the money coming in is enough to pay those bills. The Controller maintains the cash model of the company too."

"I thought that was the CFO."

"It can be, but your Chief Finance Officer is more interested in how you borrow money, your tax strategy, and how you can have the right accounting for that tax strategy whereas your controller is more interested in the day-to-day cash spending or your monthly spending. They do all the detailed analysis of your bank account. Things like: 'This is how much we have in the bank account. What do you want to do with this money? These are our pending bills, and we can choose to pay some in advance while others can be paid partially. This is our cash strategy to keep the business solvent."

"What about Procurement?"

"The Procurement role revolves around buying necessary supplies for the company. But it's essential not to centralize financial responsibilities. So, we split these finance roles. The Procurer decides what to purchase, the Controller oversees the bills, the Accounts Payable manages supplier payments, and the Accounts Receivable ensures all invoices are accurate. The Procurer essentially acts as the company's official shopper.

"To ensure a proper structure, every significant department in your business should have representation at the top level. Following that, focus on the Communications, Quality, Control, and Accounting departments, and consider adding roles like the Subcontract Manager, Pricing Specialist, and a special Procurer. Every role is crucial, regardless of your business's nature.

"Ensure you document every job your company needs. It could be a team of twenty in each department, or just one person handling everything. It all depends on your budget and growth plans. You might find that one person can handle multiple jobs, but you need to clarify each role's responsibilities to avoid any confusion.

"When hiring, focus on areas where you're not as proficient. Look for individuals whose personalities align with the roles you've defined. An accountant can be introverted or extroverted, but a salesperson needs to be an effective communicator. So, if you start with a reserved number-cruncher, you'll need to bring in an outgoing person to help you sell your products or services.

"The bottom line is that the number of people isn't as crucial as ensuring that all the essential roles are filled and well understood. Even if you're a one-person show, you can manage fifteen different tasks or more. As your business expands and you hire more help, you can delegate those responsibilities and ease your workload.

Right Butt, Right Seat

"Let's discuss how to realign workers that don't fit into the strategy. I call it 'Right Butt, Right Seat,'" I explained to Liv. "The first step to finding the right person is to define the role. I've used a simple form called the Position Qualification Sheet in several of my businesses. When managers use this form, there's no confusion about the employees' skills and their previous experiences." I easily found the form in my backpack and handed it to Liv.

Position Qualification Sheet	
Name:	
General Description: There are no "Yes" and "No" answers, except noted.	
This is where you put the General Description	Candidate please fill out the open cells below address your education, skills, qualifications, and experience to meet the requirements of this position. Can you please complete the right column with why/ how you have this experience? No Yes and NO answers please unless indicated! Our HR is evaluating candidates' qualifications against the required quals/ skills. So that's why we ask for your input
Work Authorization: Are you a US Citizen? (you can answer yes or no)	
Please list clearance or Background Check Level that must be able to possess a XXX	
Qualifications	**Qualification from Applicant**
Where/when have you performed...	
Are you a US citizen with a valid US passport? (you can answer yes or no)	

Years of Experience	
Education	
Major Duties Do not use a yes and no answers please	**Where did you perform this duty**
Required	
Skill 1	
Skill 2	
Skill 3	
Desired	
Skill 1	
Skill 2	

Fig. Position Qualification Sheet

"Using this form during the interview process can help find the right person for the job, and if there are shortcomings, you'll know up front what training requirements are needed to get the employee up to speed. You can also use this same type of process or form to identify changes due to company shifts, where employees are not a right fit."

"I can imagine it's not a pleasant conversation," she countered.

"It's true, it's tough, but it's necessary. Many people struggle to have that conversation, whether it's about reshuffling workers or even laying them off. You see, as a company grows to a team of thirty or more, there might be a few individuals who started with the business but don't fit into the current strategy anymore. We have to assess if they can be retrained and kept on board or if their role is no longer necessary. Some of these employees might possess valuable skills and knowledge, but they might not align with the direction the company is heading in."

"How do you get rid of them then without disregarding their input to the company?" Liv asked.

"Ultimately, your manner of presentation will determine how everything will go," I said. "Your choice of words is important, too. Instead of going to their desk and saying, 'You're fired, we don't need you anymore,' you can say, 'We need to talk about where you might fit or not fit in the company strategy. What can we do to help you get the job you want?'

"What scares people the most when they lose their jobs is the uncertainty that follows. They have no idea where to start looking for a new job or how long it will take them to find one. If you take that worry away from them, they will be more receptive to the change. Helping them look for a new job may or may not cost you anything. Sometimes, all it will require will be coordination with your Human Resources Department or some calls to people you know."

"Another place for relationship management," Liv noted.

"Yeah. Take the managers Steve has built a relationship with in the past two weeks. It'll be easy for him to call them and ask if any have an opening that fits the qualifications of the employee you are trying to off-ramp or move due to a restructuring. That will cost you nothing, but it will also gain you something."

"What is that?"

"An apostle. The worker will become a fan of your company because you had the option of hanging them out to dry, but you chose to help them. If that new company needs any service or products that you offer, they will be the first to say, 'Hey, my former company does that. They may even give you a good deal.' Now you're growing by word of mouth, which is the best type of growth.

"Nowadays, you hear news about a company firing twenty employees suddenly without any tangible reason. Worse still, they do it in an unprofessional manner. Then the employees start holding a protest publicly about the company and how they have been cheated. If it's a large company, like General Motors, no one will care but a small business may get ruined because of that. In business, reputation is half your selling point. You don't want to be known as the company that treats its employees like trash.

Reputation is a Relationship

"Your reputation is built on your relationships. Don't ever forget that," I emphasized.

"Tell me more about the importance of reputation. I think I haven't focused much on that aspect," Liv admitted.

"Your reputation is crucial, Liv. Working with numerous mid-size and small-scale businesses, I can attest to the fact that building and maintaining a strong reputation is as important as growing your company. A significant portion of your business comes from word-of-mouth recommendations. When someone suggests your company, potential clients often seek further confirmation, especially if substantial investments are at stake. You have no idea how many companies have deals fall through over a bottle of beer."

"They fought over a bottle of beer?" Liv asked, puzzled.

Chuckling, I clarified, "No, not literally. Imagine two managers having a casual conversation over drinks. One asks the other about your company, and depending on the feedback, the deal could either be sealed or broken. If they hear positive things about your company, they'll likely proceed. However, if they get wind of any negative incidents, it could cast doubt on your professionalism and integrity.

"Your reputation can even be tarnished by disgruntled ex-employees spreading negative rumors. It's a delicate balance that requires constant protection. Your company's culture and reputation are deeply intertwined."

"I suppose I've been cultivating it unconsciously without realizing it," Liv admitted.

Tough Conversations: Breaking Barriers to Progress

I began to pack my things back into my backpack. “There’s one other thing I wanted to talk to you about before I leave today.”

“Oh?” She asked. “What’s that?”

“It’s about Steve. We need him on board. He hasn’t bought in and this won’t work unless everyone is all in,” I told her gently. I knew I was treading on rocky grounds.

She looked at her feet. “I know,” she said softly. “I just don’t know what to say. And I don’t know how to say it.”

“I know,” I assured her. “This is really common. And if it’s alright with you, I can talk to him. You don’t have to be there.” She looked both incredibly relieved but very guilty.

“But shouldn’t I be there? Shouldn’t I be taking the responsibility?”

“In most situations, I would say yes,” I shrugged. “But damaging your personal relationship with him wouldn’t just be bad for you personally, it’d be bad for the company. And people often listen to outsiders in the way they wouldn’t listen to someone they know well.”

“Okay, because I *really* don’t want to be there for it,” she breathed out. “When do you want to do it?”

"As soon as possible. I'm going to go knock on his door now. If he's not available, it will be some other time." She watched me as I gathered my things. I could practically hear her heart thumping from where I was across the desk.

"Good luck," she called quietly after me, as I walked out of her office.

I made my way to Steve's office. The door was slightly ajar, so I knocked on it and then stuck my head in. Steve was writing on his whiteboard again. He turned around when he heard the knock.

"Brian," he was surprised to see me and not in a good way. He quickly tried to cover it up but he wasn't happy.

"Hello Steve," I started, "do you have a minute?"

"Uhhh..." I had caught him off guard. "Okay, yeah, I don't have a lot of time but come in," he said, putting the cap on the marker in his hand.

"Great, this won't take long," I said as I entered. He moved to his chair behind the desk and gestured for me to sit. "Thank you," I said as we both sat down.

I looked him directly in the eyes, not angrily, not threateningly. Just making the simple statement *I am here.*

"You need to cut the shit."

"Excuse me?" The irritation on his face was obvious.

"Do you want this company to succeed or not?"

He was completely taken aback. "Because if you do," I continued, "you need to fall in."

"Do I want this company to succeed? What a ridiculous question!" he sputtered. "I've given the last four years of my life to the company!"

"So why are you acting directly against its best interests?"

"What? Because I don't always do what you want me to do?" he asked, incredulously. "You've been here, what? Five minutes?" The energy of his anger brought him to his feet. He leaned over his desk towards me, balancing himself on his fingertips. "You look around, ask some questions and then hand down your edicts from on high and expect me just to jump to?"

Now I have to stand up too, I thought, exasperated at his one-way power struggle. "Can you *please* cut the bullshit?" I asked again, as I got to my feet. The veins on Steve's forehead looked like they would burst at any moment. "Your bad attitude and lack of cooperation are not helping move this company forward. You're not even helping this conversation move forward."

"You want me to move this conversation forward?"

"Yes, frankly," I interrupted before he could get going down that road, "I'd like you to stop blustering and stomping around like a teenager, sit down and have an adult discussion."

"How about you climb down from your high horse?" Steve started. "Four years! We built this place from nothing into a multi million-dollar company. You weren't here when we had to struggle to pay rent and our first employees. You weren't here for the ramen days when that's all we could afford to eat. Where were you when we had to figure things out by trial and error? Not here. *I* was though, Liv and I figured out how to make this company work. You just come in one day and decide everything needs to be re-shuffled according to how you want? Who the hell do you think you are?"

I kept quiet throughout his outburst. He paused to catch his breath and to pull his tie away from his neck. "I told Liv we could figure this out on our own, but she had to bring you in," grumbling resentfully.

He was pacing up and down the office but he didn't seem to have anything else to say.

"Are you done?" I finally asked.

"I'm done," he said, he turned around, not knowing what to do with himself. The couch caught his eye, so he went over and sat on it.

I turned my chair around and sat down facing him. "Okay, Steve, you did a great job getting this company to where it is. We can both agree on that, right?" I asked. He looked at me suspiciously but only nodded.

"Yes, you did," I said. "You did it. You grew a multi-million dollar company. You should be really proud of yourself." I watched him watching me, waiting for the other shoe to drop.

"But it's not growing anymore. You figured out how to get it to where it is, but it has to be obvious to you now that you have absolutely no idea how to grow it further. It's obvious to everyone else." He scowled, I went on regardless. "And there's no shame in that. None! What there is shame in is being an obstinate fool who is so blinded by his own insecurities that he lets that company he and his friend put all their blood, sweat and tears into to build, stagnate and die...just for pride and spite."

Steve's jaw dropped. He just sat there, stunned.

"If you're being honest with yourself, you know what I'm saying is true." I chided him. "And that's why you're getting so upset."

He stared at me and I just calmly looked back at him, for a good 30 seconds. Then he looked up at the ceiling and fell back into the couch, a huge breath *whooshing* out of him.

He stared up at the ceiling for several more moments. He closed his eyes, stuck his thumbs in the inner corners of them and started to shake his head.

"You're right," he said. "You're right." He let his hands fall and just kept staring at the ceiling.

"Yes, you built this company, you got it to the level it's at. I'm here to help you get it to the next level. Help me do that," I implored him. "Let's work together to do that."

Without moving his body, he set his eyes on me. I was surprised to see a tear in one of them.

"Okay, Steve. You are not the only one who has given his all to the business. Look at this picture." I showed him a picture from Liv's table of her in her Army uniform.

"You can see how she looked like someone happy and free from worries. Look at that bright face and her light demeanor. Now compare that to her now. You both have given your all to the company. I don't know about you, but she has no backup plan. If this business fails, she has nothing to fall back on."

"Liv does not deserve this. It was her dream to start this place. She would not talk about anything else. I begged her to let me share that dream. Tell me, Brian, have I ruined everything?"

"Steve, you haven't ruined anything yet, but things will be ruined if we continue this way. You are a critical part of this business..."

"Everything I have is in this place."

"I'm here to help you too. It is not you against me. We are on the same team." He closed his eyes and nodded slowly.

"And hey," I told him with a smile, "I would be remiss if I didn't admit that you got me good. You really impressed me with all the work you've done in rekindling your relationships with your clients."

He let out a laugh, "I showed you, huh?"

"Yes, you did."

"I was just so—" he started.

"I know," I said. "I know you were."

He smiled again. "Thanks," came out like a whisper.

"This is your baby, Steve," I told him, getting up, "I am here to help you grow it to be the best it can be."

He stood up to see me out.

"Thanks for the kick in the ass," he smiled as we shook hands.

"Anytime," I chuckled, as I went through the door.

I stepped into the hallway and saw Liv's face peeking out of her office. I smiled and gave her a thumbs up. It looked like eight years fell away from her face. "Thank you," she said. I waved goodbye. "You're welcome," I replied as I turned and walked away.

CHAPTER SIX
THE BOND BEYOND BUSINESS

Liv wasn't kidding when she said Steve was good with people. His eager handshake made me feel like we had been friends for years even though our new alliance was only three days old. It was clear how quickly he could put a person at ease.

I could already sense the palpable energy the moment Liv and I stepped into the conference room. I had set up a meeting with Steve and his team. He greeted me with a familiar, warm smile, and a handshake that spoke of old hurdles crossed and new bridges built. "Brian, glad you made it. Meet the core of our operations."

Julie, Dan, and Roy offered friendly nods and smiles. We briefly shared light-hearted stories of weekend getaways, favorite movies, and the latest books we'd read. Simple, yet meaningful conversations. It's those moments of genuine human interaction that lay the foundation for trust and understanding in any professional relationship.

The gentle sound of the door interrupted our chatter as Liv walked in. Her presence was always reassuring. She exchanged pleasantries, then looked my way, a silent cue to get started.

"I appreciate the warm welcome," I began, "Today, we are going to talk about the foundation for all good business development: relationships.

"Think about it this way—who do you think our main customers are? Well, let me tell you who they're not—your enemies. Your customers are either those who trust you or those who want to get to know you. Your enemies don't fall into either of those groups. So, the real difference between making impressive sales and not-so-impressive ones is how well you can build solid relationships with these customers."

"Is that what you mean by 'relationship management'?" asked Liv.

"Exactly," I said. "Managing your relationships with clients is crucial. This includes understanding how to find great sales representatives, or even how to become one yourself. Let's focus on making sure that the sales representatives really understand what they're selling, get why it's important for the customer to be happy with the product, and know how to build a strong bond of loyalty and commitment with the buyer. Remember, building a strong team and nurturing relationships is what will drive the growth you're looking for."

The Ideal Business Development Team—Relationships, Experience and Insight

"But before we delve deeper into strategy, I want to ask you a question: In your opinion, what truly defines a successful business development?"

"A great salesperson is driven by belief in the product or service they're selling," offered Julie. "They need to know it inside out and be convinced that it's exactly what the buyer needs and how it can help them in their processes, even if the buyer isn't aware of it yet."

"Yes, but that's not always the case," I responded. "You have to do your research. The buyer might not be aware of their need, but it's our responsibility to demonstrate that we are the solution. Our task is to build the case for why the buyer should trust us enough to choose our business. It often becomes a trade-off within their budget. To make the sale, we might need to displace something else.

"On top of that, this motivation doesn't stop once the customer makes a purchase. It continues even after the sale is finalized. The team should be motivated by the client's satisfaction with their purchase and the deal we've offered. If there's any issue with the product or service, the team should be capable of finding a solution. That's how we establish a foundation of trust and dependability, isn't it? It's all about the relationship!"

Steve and Liv nodded in agreement, while Julie and Dan echoed, "Absolutely."

"I hadn't considered it from that angle before," Roy added.

"Another characteristic you should never underestimate is a person's dedication and loyalty to the company as well as their passion for their job. A professional with no passion and loyalty for their job is only setting themselves and the company up for failure. Dedicated professionals get up on a cold December morning and get out of their warm, comfy bed to go to yet another meeting with a client. It's why a salesperson will spend hours stuck in traffic just because they have another client to meet on the other side of town. They will do tedious work without complaining. As leaders we want to strive to get that level of dedication, loyalty, and passion. It is what you want to see in your employees. It is their desire to do their best every day that makes the difference."

"I have a question, Brian," Liv interrupted.

"Shoot."

"The last time we spoke, we talked about my strategy, how to create the three-to-five-year targets and how to build my team. So, is this the step where we should identify what skills the salespeople need to have so we hire the right person?"

"Yes, it is," I said. "In fact, it is one of the first things you need to consider before starting the hiring process. The salesperson ought to be compatible with your company's strategy. That is how you can be sure they will fit into your overall plan for the business. You can't hire a big process product sales representative for a boutique services company, right? Their skill set does not match. A boutique services company is concerned about selling now because their goods are ready in their stores, but a big process company may not be in delivery for twelve or eighteen months. It's a different ball game altogether which requires long-term relationship management.

"Another important thing to look out for is how well the salesperson understands the product they are selling. This is to make sure that they can efficiently sell it to a buyer. You can't give out what you don't have. If they don't understand it, they can't explain it to the buyer either. I would say you are not a proper sales representative until you can explain your product to a fifth grade student.

"The credibility of the salesperson you hire is a bonus to the company too. It could take years to build it, but there are people who are recognized due to their experience in the industry. They've spent all their lives building their reputation as experts in their field. Their names alone can open doors. When they walk in to pitch your company to a client, their impressive background speaks volumes.

"Now these experienced individuals are *highly* motivated people. They have skin in the game; they have something to lose. They've spent a long time building their reputation so it's in their own best interest to build strong, foundational relationships with your clients. They will make sure your products satisfy the customers because their reputation is on the line."

"If they have invested a lot into their reputation, won't they be expensive?" Dan asked.

"That's a good point," I replied. "They do require higher compensation, which is why I almost always advise business owners to pay sales reps on performance pay."

"A lot of reps require a salary," Steve commented.

"Some sales cycles are longer to process so you might need a smaller base with a commission. But if all they are worried about is their base salary, then you can be sure they are not very good sales reps. Any sales rep worth their salt would bet on themselves. Especially if there's no limit to what they can earn. Plus, who you don't hire is as important as who you do hire. There is a type of sales rep that you should keep away from—the robotic ones. You know the type. They try to sell things to you but all they do is recite the product description. A buyer can sense when your salesperson is working from a script. The sales reps won't be able to answer the questions the customers would ask. Anyone who has hired robotic sales reps will tell you the same thing I'm telling you right now—stay away from them!

"You need to consider the importance of experience over education too. For instance, Liv, did Todd tell you about my PhD when he recommended me?"

"No, he didn't."

"That's because my clients value my experience and the results I have had in the marketplace, not the fancy letters that come after my name. This is how you should evaluate most hires. There should be a conscious effort to ensure you have the right experience and the right education. Experience may trump education in many cases. Your clients will respect your reps based on the practical expertise they have, not by how many degrees they have listed from whatever schools are on their resumé."

"You know, Brian, you've been talking about these sales reps like they are outgoing people. What about introverts who have no social skills?" Liv asked.

"If you have no social skills, we do not need you in the business development team. I know there are some outliers but a person in your BD team has to be able to get out there and talk, mingle and promote with confidence. Again, it all goes back to relationships. Business Development is about building relationships. You can't do that if you don't have the ability to connect with people. Your team should be able to earn a customer's trust after talking to them. Sales Representatives need people to like them. Relationship management for individuals in your sales department requires a lot of networking and listening, because they will be the face of the company at happy hour, conventions, events, or attending games to meet clients.

"There should never be rudeness from sales reps, no matter what. They should be the people clients want to have coffee with. There should be handshakes, bear hugs, and deep talks to foster trust. Your trust should be deep enough for them to call you first when there's a mistake with their purchase instead of throwing it at your doorstep the next day."

"So, you want us to build a formal relationship?" Steve asked.

"Not too formal for them to invite you to be their son's godfather, but meaningful enough for them to share good news in their life when you meet."

Everyone nodded.

"So, those are the main things you need to consider before hiring a sales representative. Your requirements will depend on your strategy and how you want them to fit into the company's plans."

"You look confused, Steve," I said. "What part isn't clear?"

"Well, you talked about getting close to the client, but you didnt' say anything about how to take the first step towards getting close to them. I have dealt with clients, and I know the first step is the hardest."

"You're right, the first step is the hardest, which is another reason you should research the client before you meet them. Your assignment starts before you even get close to them. We also must identify who are the right people in the organization to reach out to for contact.

"Once we know who the right people are, you need touchpoints to make conversations with them. You should visit their LinkedIn or other social media pages to find out their interests. Also, if you find common friends you can ask them about the other person. You may have taken the same classes or even supported the same football team. They could own a pet, just like you. Any of those things create a basis for a conversation that starts to build a relationship.

"One final thing that drives the type of relationship between a sales representative and the client is the type of product being sold.

"OK, let's use OBIDA Global as an example. If the client is buying data services from the sales rep, for instance, then it needs to be a close relationship because things can change quickly. If something changes in the delivery pipeline, the sales rep needs to know as soon as possible because the official information may be too late. An increase in the client's needs will lead to more product deliveries so the sales rep needs to have first-hand information on that. Not to mention, various scenarios within the client's company can impact the delivery of our data products to them, despite being unnoticed by the outside world."

Capturing Customer Requirements

"Next, I want to discuss the concept of 2/2/1. The basics of business say that one party sells to the other party, right?"

"Yes," Steve and Liv answered at the same time.

"So what is 2/2/1?" Dan asked.

"It means you should use your two ears, two eyes, and one mouth wisely," I explained. "Then you're naturally equipped to absorb more information. Listen to the customers, observe them, and as you discuss ways to fulfill their needs, maintain good communication. When we get this part right, we start the relationship on the right foot. We're building rapport, showing the customer we understand their needs, and can provide valuable recommendations before moving on to deliver a product that meets their requirements.

"The next step after this is to bring in a Technical Writer," I continued. "Their role is to document all your client's requirements accurately. This documentation is vital for creating a proposal request or the final contract.

"It's similar to a real estate transaction," I added. "You hire a skilled salesperson who convinces me that you're a talented builder, and I hire you to construct my dream house. Once we agree on the terms, our business relationship begins. Then, you pass me on to your design team, or as we call them in business, 'Capture.' I can specify that I want a three-bedroom house, yellow paint, specific tiles, and a 3,500-square-foot layout. The Technical Writer records all these details, and it becomes an agreement when you've figured out how to build it, its cost, and my payment plan. This agreement eventually turns into a contract that both you and I sign, solidifying our agreement to do business together."

Network and Negotiations

"However, none of the strategies we've discussed will be effective if we can't attract the clients. You understand that, right? Cultivating and managing relationships alone isn't sufficient to draw in these clients, unfortunately.

"You may have come across the familiar tale of a sales representative who can spark interest in ten people using a single line, yet struggles to seal the deal. It's a common challenge for some sales reps and business developers. They can generate interest in their products and maintain relationships, but they face difficulty in persuading these potential clients to make a purchase."

"Actually," Roy interjected, "I have a problem closing."

"I do, too," Dan said.

"Me too," Julie added.

"Well," I said, "this means your company does not have a Closer, Liv."

A sudden lull fell upon the room and everyone leaned back on their seats as if they had been defeated yet again.

"Oh, come on," I said, "This doesn't take anything away from your capability. It only means that Liv now may have to hire another person for the Business Development team or work with this team to enhance that skill."

I started to flip through my notes, but a thought ran through my mind. I paused and looked at Steve. "Uhh… Steve?"

"Yes?" He answered.

"How have you been doing your pitches all this time?"

"Uh…I give the targets and the assignments out to the team as soon as I find one. Then each member builds their proposal from the research they conduct on the client."

"Then?"

"They come to me with the proposal, and I do the rest."

"So, you are the Closer!"

He didn't know the term but yes he had been doing it the whole time.

"Ah, you're aware that this approach would imply that the other team members aren't being trained to close deals for the future, right?"

"I know that now, but I want to be involved in that final decision-making process."

"I need to tell you something, Steve. You can't oversee everything. We have to establish a system where other team members can take on that role.

"OK, here's what we're going to do. Steve will handle the closing for now, and he'll collaborate with the rest of the team when finalizing a deal. If we keep hiring more people, you'll soon reach your capacity limit. Even if you train them, how will you monitor them when you're already swamped?

"But here's the good news. We'll discuss how to ensure accountability within your team later[11] so that you won't have to constantly supervise them to ensure they're following the given directives. Remember, the aim for every Business Development team is to bid less and win more! But for now, let's continue our focus on relationship management.

Relationship Management

"We'll keep talking about how to handle relationships with everyone involved in your business, like clients, target companies, vendors, employees, and investors. It's important to maintain good relationships with all these people. As you grow, you can get into managing relationships with the board and shareholders, but let's stick to clients for now. There are a few things you need to take care of to make sure the company has a good relationship with the clients, especially in your Business Development department.

11 See Chapter 7

Understanding The Client

"Understanding the client is crucial. You need to know:

- What they want
- What they don't want
- How they think
- Whether you'll need to make concessions for them
- Where the common ground is between the two companies.

"Before you can meet your clients' needs, you have to truly understand them. Don't rush into satisfying them right away. Some sales representatives or business developers make the mistake of presenting the price upfront. What's the hurry? You might end up competing against yourself.

"The client might be taken aback by the price, causing confusion. They'll start questioning everything you've told them. 'Why is this so expensive? Do we really need this?' It can get messy. Before you even discuss pricing, you should have a deep understanding of what they require. We'll delve into this further in the MAN Process, but remember, discussing pricing shouldn't be a faceless exchange. It's essential to have this conversation with someone who understands the client or has the closest relationship with them.

"What if the client can't afford it? The sales rep or the business development representative can sit down with the client to work out a solution. You can help them remove what they definitely can't afford. Be careful not to cut too much, as it might lead them to question the validity of the pricing proposal."

Integration of Relationship Management into Strategy

"The next thing you need to do for your clients is to integrate this relationship management into your strategy. Your strategy should contain the important parts of your business. By including it in the strategy, you would have given it a form of legitimacy. People—by that I mean big companies—always talk about integrating relationships into the strategy but I always say that the relationship you have with your clients is the buying strategy."

"People don't buy from enemies," Steve recalled.

"That's correct," I said.

"How come we never thought about all of this?" Liv asked, throwing her hands up.

The laughter that filled the conference room released the tension that had been building since the beginning of the meeting.

Maintaining a Balance in Client Dependability

"Let me ask you about the computers in your office," I said, changing the topic. "How did you purchase them? Chances are, a salesman from a tech retail company downstairs, Tom I believe you said, handled that for you. If one of your monitors suddenly malfunctions, who would you call for repairs within the warranty period? That's right, you'd call Tom.

"Tom is the closest point of contact in his company for you. He's the one who upholds the relationship between his company and yours. If you voice a complaint to him, will Tom himself come over with a screwdriver to fix it? No, he won't. He'll coordinate with the appropriate department in his company, and they'll come to assess the situation. However, when you call him, you expect immediate attention to your problem because you trust he'll be there for you.

"It's up to Tom to respond promptly and resolve your issues when you reach out. This availability is crucial. If he disregards your complaint calls repeatedly, you might reconsider buying from him the next time he pitches a great sales opportunity from his company.

"The same principle applies to your company. When your clients call, you answer. This is how you manage relationships. Show them they can always rely on you to be there whenever they need assistance. When you present a new product to them next time, you won't have to ask twice."

Eliminating Complacency and Improving Habits

"When it comes to your clients, it's essential to steer clear of complacency and negative habits. Take Steve, for instance, who became somewhat complacent after securing the first clients for the firm. That should never happen again. You should always stay sharp and ready.

"Steve began assuming what the clients wanted rather than understanding their needs, losing his edge. The thing about relationship management is that your bad habits can work against you. If you have a penchant for gambling, it's crucial to keep it in check. I wouldn't trust a company with a gambling addict handling their finances or a vital department like Business Development. If you have a habit of being late, ensure you're always punctual for meetings with your clients. Remember the significance of making a strong first and lasting impression.

"We want clients to remember us well beyond the first meeting. So, our aim is to foster more successful interactions while reducing unnecessary bids. In our next relationship management plan, let's explore the blocking and tackling strategy."

Liv tilted her head and asked, "Like the football strategy?"

I nodded. "The blocking and tackling strategy is a systematic approach to relationship management that emphasizes thorough research and understanding of clients before engaging with them. You should have done your research, understand the company and your role in their overall mission and success. I've heard clients complain, 'The new sales guy showed up, but he didn't even know what we do.' Don't be that sales representative who remains clueless about the client's management or leadership."

Opportunity Matrix

"We are about to talk about the opportunity matrix. Now, I can assume that everyone understands the meaning of opportunity in business—the "O" in SWOT. It's that thing they say comes but once. Like every other part of business, opportunity is golden. When you properly use it, the result can be amazing. The opportunity matrix we'll be talking about is how you can take advantage of the various opportunities your buyers will give to you. Let's take a look at the handouts I gave you".

Opportunity Matrix			
Quadrant		Quadrant	
I. Existing Customer/ Existing Capability		III. New Customer/ Existing Capability	
II. Existing Customer/ New Capability		IV. New Customer/ New Capability	

Fig. The Opportunity Matrix

"In this chart, you can see the different customer segments you should focus on and how you can keep them satisfied with your products. It's known as The Four Quadrants.

The Four Quadrants

"They are the quadrants that your opportunity as a company can be divided into:

1. Quadrant One: Current customer, existing capability
2. Quadrant Two: Existing customer, new capability
3. Quadrant Three: New customer, existing capability
4. Quadrant Four: New customer, new capability."

"How is this our opportunity matrix, Brian?" Liv questioned.

"Let's go through them one by one," I said.

Quadrant One: Current Customer, New Capability

"Quadrant One represents the opportunity with your existing customers who already make purchases from your business. These individuals are already buying your products, and the goal is to encourage them to buy more. If you treat them well, they'll likely be open to expanding their purchases from you. Remember when I mentioned the possibility of your company missing out on potential revenue? These are the customers who have the potential to increase their spending with you."

Quadrant Two: Existing Customer, New Capability

"The second quadrant involves current customers to whom you're introducing a new product or service. Just the other day, when I spoke with Jim, I realized that this quadrant has been overlooked for quite some time. Apart from your business intelligence and data analytics, you haven't introduced any new offerings to your current customer base or maybe there are other departments in the company that can use our services.

"When you maintain strong relationships with your clients, you'll have team members who can let you know about a new need that can be fulfilled. Recognizing this need makes it easier to present the new offering to the client, especially because they have already made a purchase from you. If you've been consistently reliable throughout the initial sale, they'll be more inclined to consider the next service from you. Once you succeed in selling this new solution, you'll be on the path to significant growth before you know it."

Quadrant Three: New Customer, Existing Capability

"The third quadrant involves the core function of sales representatives, which is to introduce your product to new customers. This is where you can use different approaches to connect with them: 'Hey, we're skilled at business analysis, and we've been doing it successfully. If you inquire about us, you'll find our reputation is excellent.' 'We're good, but we haven't had the chance to work with you yet. Let's grab some coffee and discuss how we can assist you with this capability we have.' 'I noticed the Army sticker on your car. It's impressive, as I served some time ago.'

"We'll revisit this topic when we discuss the MAN in a minute, focusing on how to identify this type of person and how to approach them. We've already talked about using networks to initiate these conversations. While this quadrant may not yield as much success as the first two, flipping some clients here can significantly boost your growth. Remember, without gaining new customers, you won't have any existing customers. Of course, new clients eventually become long-term patrons."

Quadrant Four: New Customer, New Capability

"The fourth quadrant is the hardest of the lot. I call it the home run quadrant. Here, you do not understand the customer. They've never bought from you before. All you know is that they are a buyer of business intelligence, but you want to sell a new product to them. So we are taking the big swing."

"How do you sell to them?" Steve asked.

"You do the homework. We have to figure them out before approaching. Closing will be harder because you'll have to convince them to give you money without a proven track record of you or the new product you're trying to sell. I'm not worried about this quadrant. I'm more worried about the mistakes people usually make."

"What mistakes?" Liv asked.

"Too many times, I see clients in this quadrant burning money and time on the highest risk quadrant. Let's say you have three new customers that you've been chasing around with your new capability in the fourth quadrant. You could easily introduce that new capability to the existing customer in quadrant two, right? Spreading your selling goals across these four quadrants will make it easier for you to achieve them. So, let's take a look at that quadrant again and fill some of it in."

Opportunity Matrix			
Quadrant		Quadrant	
I. Existing Customer/ Existing Capability	• XYZ Inc. (DA) • International Inc. (BI)	III. New Customer/ Existing Capability	• Humana (DA) • Tricore (BI)
II. Existing Customer/ New Capability	??	IV. New Customer/ New Capability	• ACME Testing (Enhanced DA) • Beneficial Govt (Enhanced BI) • Stalmart (Enhanced BI

"How do we sell to people in these quadrants? I understand the importance of maintaining relationships with them, but how do we identify the right person to foster these relationships with? Who exactly is the Key Influencer?"

Identifying Key Influencers: Finding the MAN

"It's a question every business owner asks: 'How do I get this company to buy from me?' I kid you not, business is about who you know. So, you must know the right people and the key influencers in your target companies—someone who is in the decision-making circle or knows the person that is in the circle.

"Let's say we've created our strategy. We've also identified the target we're going for. The next thing we should find out is how that company buys. Do they have a department of acquisition? Who signs off on where they buy from? To answer these questions, you need to find the MAN."

"That's a little sexist," Liv commented flatly.

"No! It's an acronym."

"Oh!" she said.

The MAN (Money, Authority, Need)

"The M stands for Money. In other words, who in the organization controls the money? Sometimes the money in an organization is held centrally. At other times, it is decentralized.

"Then A means Authority. Who has the power to approve spending this money? Do they have standard contracting officers in-house, or do they have buyers in each division that decide for the business director? How's the organization built to spend the money?

"The last part, N, is for Need. Here, we're concerned about the end user, right? This is the person who would use our product. They are the ones we gather data from to make sure our product is successful, and it gives them what they need. In your case, this is the person who wants data analysis from you.

"If you know all three people involved in the transaction, it's easier to build the relationship and understand how your buyer is thinking and how they would use your product.

"In a different company, I presented this example and connected it to following the money. At the end of the presentation, the VP for Business Development looked at me and said, 'I've been doing this for 20 years, and you made it seem so simple. I feel like a rookie.'"

Influencing Key Influencers Using the MAN Approach

I passed around a hand-out that had the blank MAN chart.

Who is the MAN?				
Key Customers Decision Makers				
Organization	**Lead**	**Money (M)**	**Authority (A)**	**Need (N) End User**
XYZ Inc.	Steve	John	Sam	Ben
International Inc.	Roy			
Humana	Julie			
Tricore	Julie			
ACME Testing	Dan			
Beneficial Govt	Dan			
Stalmart	Dan			
Key Stakeholders				
Key Decision	**Issue/ Hot Button/ Need**	**Weight (1-10)**		

Fig. The MAN Chart

"Now, Steve, with what we've just discussed, can you fill out those blank spaces?"

"The ones about the MAN?"

"Yes, exactly," I said.

Steve began to list the individuals that filled the roles.

The new chart looked like this:

Who is the MAN?				
Key Customers Decision Makers				
Organization	**Lead**	**Money (M)**	**Authority (A)**	**Need (N) End User**
XYZ Inc.	Steve	John	Sam	Ben
International Inc.	Roy	Various	Suzy	Sarah
Humana	Julie			
Tricore	Julie		SE Contract Officer (??)	
ACME Testing	Dan			
Beneficial Govt	Dan			
Stalmart	Dan			
Key Stakeholders				
Key Decision	**Issue/ Hot Button/ Need**	**Weight (1-10)**		

Fig. Who is the MAN?

"Great, Steve. You've identified them correctly. According to this chart, you understand that John holds the money, Sam functions as the Contract Officer or the Buying Agent, and Ben is the person you receive your requirements from. You've identified International Inc. as a current customer and Roy as the Lead. Susie serves as the Contract Officer, and Sarah is the end user. However, it seems we're missing information about the source of the funding. Julie and Dan, can you complete the charts as your homework?"

"Yes, we'll complete it," Julie said, "but how do I look for this MAN? Steve and Roy have been with their clients for years, but I don't have an existing relationship with these companies yet. Where do I start?"

Comprehensive Understanding of Targets

"I normally start by figuring out my first point of contact. Usually, it's the buyer because it's easier to find out who's been buying from a company. So, your first goal is to find the person with the Need. They are the ones pulsing the network for who they should look at or who they should use. You could use LinkedIn and other mediums to find out who works in the target company. The business world is a small one, especially since this is a company you're selling to. You will find someone who has something in common with you. They don't need to have the pull, but they can introduce you to the person who does. I call this person a 'Key Influencer.' A key influencer can provide you an initial introduction and also help build some key points to begin a conversation with a person. It is our way of getting a personal touch point to begin a relationship.

"This introduction is way better than cold calling. Think about your receptionist Kerry, you'd likely trust who she introduces to you more than you would trust someone who emailed you without a connection. You could even get lucky and get introduced to the Money guy before you meet the Need guy.

"Before meeting anyone new, make sure to do your homework. Think of it like doing a research paper back in school. Get to know who they are and how their company works. This way, you can understand their problems and figure out how your product can be the solution."

"How effective is this MAN approach?" asked

"Look at it this way, let's say you want to pitch a brilliant idea to Stall Mart, which could significantly help their business process. What you want to avoid doing is running to Stall Mart, giving fifteen briefs, and never engaging with any member of the MAN. You might speak to a junior engineer there who may like your presentation, but they likely don't have the authority to seal the deal. Even if the junior engineer's manager likes your presentation, they still might not be part of the authority matrix. You could end up conducting hundreds of presentations within the organization without having a clear idea of how they intend to proceed after showing interest in your pitch."

Strategies in Motion

As the rest of the team left the meeting, I gathered my notes and packed my backpack. Liv and Steve fell into step behind me as we left the room.

"I had a proposal I was working on for a new client, Brian," Steve said.

"Really?" I raised an eyebrow

"I'm tearing it up once I get back to my office."

"Why?" Liv asked.

"I thought I'd attend the opening ceremony for the company upstairs tomorrow night instead."

"Isn't that party invitation only?" asked Liz.

"I'll call Tom, the computer guy, he always gets invited to this sort of thing. I can bet that he'll have a potential guest list too."

"What will you do, Steve?" I asked him.

"I'll put everything you taught us today into practice. First, I'll make a call to Tom. I'll research those guests. Tomorrow night, I'll do what I do best."

"Which is?"

"Winning hearts and minds, Brian. Winning hearts and minds."

We walked a few feet before Steve started to pull back.

"Brian, I need to get back into my flow with work. Hopefully, I'll have good news for you the next time you're here, which is when exactly?"

"Let's give it two weeks this time. Good luck, Steve."

"Thank you," he replied and shook my hand.

He started back to the office as Liv followed me to my truck. "I'll work on what we discussed today with Steve. I can assure you that you'll see differences the next time you're here."

"I don't doubt that. I'll keep in touch with your progress. Tell Steve I'll always be ready to offer my advice if he needs any during that time."

"That's a lot of work to take on," she said.

"Yeah, it's kind of my job."

"That's why I pay you the big bucks!"

I laughed and waved goodbye.

CHAPTER SEVEN

ESTABLISHING GOALS AND ENSURING ACCOUNTABILITY:

SETTING METRICS, MANAGING RELATIONSHIPS, AND ACHIEVING SUCCESS

One morning, more than a week after my relationship management meeting with Liv's Business Development team, my phone's ringtone jolted me from my sleep. I was three time zones away from Tampa, and I hadn't put my phone on silent.

I answered with a groggy, "Hello?"

"Hi, Brian," Liv's voice came through on the other end of the line. Her tone instantly woke me up.

"Oh, Liv. Are you alright?"

"I don't know," she answered.

"What do you mean you don't know? Is everything alright? You don't sound like yourself."

"I still don't know how I'm feeling right now, Brian. I've dreamt and hoped for this day for years now. It's finally here, and I don't know what to feel."

I checked my phone to confirm it was indeed Liv calling. This did not sound like the straight-to-the-point business-person I knew.

"What are you talking about, Liv?"

"Someone just left my office."

"Okay?"

"They wanted to open an account with us."

I stifled the yawn that was about to escape my mouth.

"What?"

"We have a new client, Brian. After all this time, we finally got a new one!"

"That is great news!."

I had anticipated this happening but not so fast. It had only been a few weeks since my talk on relationship management. How did the team do it so fast?

"Hello? Brian? Are you there?"

"Yes, I am Liv. Congratulations!"

"I mean, it's not a done deal yet but someone walked into my office to set up an account. Steve gave me a heads up, but I didn't know it would happen that fast."

"Tell me everything," I said as sat up.

She explained that Steve had gone to that opening ceremony and started a relationship with three potential clients there. Tom, the guy they buy their computers from, introduced him to them as regular clients. Tom also gave them a glowing recommendation. Steve put his relationship management skills to work as I had told him.

"It's your first true growth, you should be happy," I said.

Reluctantly she said, "I am. It's just so… you know what I mean?"

In fact, I did. She was stunned.

"You should be proud of your Business Development team, Liv. That's gold you have right there," I reminded her.

"Thank you, Brian. I should get back to work," she said, and we hung up.

I could not go back to sleep after that call. My head was

spinning with new ideas and opportunities. Our work was paying off already.

Aligning Goals with Realities

A week later, I was in Liv's office, sipping on a latte while she told me about another client they had closed. She was clearly thrilled. She invited me to the dinner she was hosting for her team later that night, but I had another commitment already booked.

"Liv, you can't imagine how glad I am that you're receiving your results this fast. Let's just make sure not to get complacent. This is a fragile time."

"I understand your concern, Brian," she said. "What are we talking about today?"

"We already spoke about this earlier but in light of your recent achievement, I believe it's time to bring it back again. This time, we will match it with what we spoke about the last time I was in your company—the art of goal setting. We talked about setting goals for yourself and how fast you want your company to grow, and how to make sure you match your strategy with your goal. This time, I want to talk to you about how you should align your goals with your existing capabilities."

"Okay, Brian. Let's start," she replied eagerly.

"The first time we talked about your goals, Liv, we mentioned that you wanted a hundred percent growth within the next three years, right?"

"Right. I passed that on to Steve's and Jim's teams too," she clarified.

"That was before we talked about quadrants and the importance of relationship management. Now, you need to plan out how you will achieve that goal. You need to start deciding where in the four quadrants you want to see the growth. How do you want to see it? How do you want to enhance your relationship with your current customers and the new ones you just got? It's okay if you don't have these answers yet, Liv. It's fine if you need to think about it. You can't afford complacency at this stage you're in now. You can't afford to let employees run wild on their own yet either. So, you need accountability. You need to apply the principles of setting metrics that we talked about in the past with the principles of the four quadrants and relationship management," I instructed.

"I should set goals in the four quadrants to hold my employees accountable for how much they've achieved in each?" she responded as she remembered our previous conversation.

"Exactly. This way, you can go back to Steve and say, 'Hey, I need a hundred percent growth in the entire company. You need to achieve twenty percent of that growth. This is what twenty percent of that growth looks like to your company.' Then you can go to Jim and say, 'Hey, I want your guys to start presenting advanced data analysis to our existing customers so we can build a proper relationship with them,' I said.

"It's important at this point that you be as clear as you can be with your staff. Clarity is essential in goal setting. You don't want the excuse of not achieving a goal to be that your message wasn't properly communicated."

"Where does the MAN come into this goal setting?" she asked.

"It has been helpful to me, and my clients in the past, to create a goal achievement path through the MAN matrix," I explained.

"How?"

"You saw the chart I told the BD team to fill out two weeks ago, right? You'll tell them to use that sort of chart for every target they are pursuing. Through that, you can now be specific about who you want them to meet and when they should meet them. Do you understand?" I could sense she was struggling.

"I'm getting there," she answered.

I went on to explain, "There is a difference between your team briefing you about a target and them saying, 'Liv, I'm going to see the Southern Contracting officer.' That will allow you to ask, 'Okay, Jim. What's the deadline for their production? When are you planning to deliver their product?' If your guy says, 'Oh, I have no idea yet but it's coming along,' you can reply with, 'I want it done in two weeks, not as soon as possible.' See? You've created accountability. They won't get complacent because you know everything. You know *who* they are meeting. You know *when* they are meeting that person."

"Honestly, Brian, I think this is too much information at once," she said.

"Okay, we can break it down a bit more. Let's talk about the goals and their alignment with different departments in your company. We'll break down the information so that you can follow it clearly, right? So, the first part is aligning goals with your contracts."

Aligning Goals With Contracts

"You're a business owner so you know what a contract means. Essentially, it's how you make your money and build your company. If you want to achieve the goals you've set for your business, you need to align those goals with whatever contract you're dealing with at any given moment, whether it's a government contract or a commercial contract. You need to ask when your customers buy and what time of year your sales are higher.

"Your goals and strategy should match when your customers are buying. When they buy from you, is it a seasonal or a cyclical buy? If you've done government contracts before, you'd know that the biggest buy will be in the third quarter. Your goal here is to align your measurable goals against the buyer's buying cycles. I have watched too many companies set goals that don't make sense. It tells me the owner or leader has business training but has not applied common sense."

As I explained this to Liv, I could see she was beginning to understand. I went on to explain aligning goals with the four quadrants.

Aligning Goals with The Four Quadrants

"Based on my experience, quadrants one and two are where you will see the easiest growth because these clients already know you, right? Two and three, however, are where you should set the biggest target."

I showed her their quadrant chart to refresh her memory that:

- Quadrant one is existing customers, existing capability.
- Quadrant two is existing customers, new capability.
- Quadrant three, new client, existing capability.
- Quadrant four, new customer, new capability.

"These quadrants are the keys that will unlock your true growth. Remember not to focus too much on one and abandon the others. As I mentioned before, many companies concentrate heavily on acquiring clients from the fourth quadrant and neglect the second.

"I recommend going back, looking at your commercial and government customers, figuring out what their cycles are, and then readjusting to client cycles so that you can focus on the quadrants and quarters you need to focus on. It'll also help you to focus on delivery. I'm sure I don't have to remind you of the time saved through proper goal setting in these quadrants.

"When you build relationships and do thorough homework on the MAN, you save time. Finding the key people to talk to and establishing a strong relationship upfront helps you work efficiently. You'll avoid spending time chasing after unlikely opportunities or briefing individuals not involved in the decision-making process, as you set specific goals with a clear strategy."

Who Calls the Shots?

"Okay," Liv said slowly as she thought. "So every department needs a specific goal and strategy. It would make sense then that Steve, Jim, and Susan talk with their team and then come back to me with their goals."

"Sort of," I explained. "Too many cooks spoil the broth. You want to avoid the confusion that contradictions can cause within your company. It's your responsibility to set goals but everyone will contribute towards *realizing* those goals."

"Hmm," she nodded in agreement.

"As the boss, you're on top of it all. Your job is to give them the goal. Tell them where you want to be and what quadrants you need to see growth in. Your managers, directors, or the Vice President—when you eventually get one—would then work on how to realize that. They would go back to their subordinates and say, 'The boss said she wants forty-five percent of our growth to be in quadrant three. How can we achieve that? Is that realizable or do we need to shift it a little?' If the boots on the ground have any reservations about that goal, they send their concern to your managers who get back to you again."

"One up, two down," she offered.

"Yes, ma'am. Your managers will set smaller goals because you need to set these bigger goals too. For instance, the President and Joint Chiefs of Staff can say, 'By December, we have to surround so and so country for such and such reasons.' It is the Generals who then plan out the strategy of taking that country, but the Commanding Officer of a company or battalion will focus on the city or an important infrastructure his men have been tasked to take. When the battle starts, each squad leader or platoon leader—or business managers and team leaders—must take care of their men and create tactics that will direct them on what they should do to take that city. Platoon A could be in charge of holding the bridge while Platoon B is in charge of clearing the buildings.

"So, the planning starts from the top, right? From the President to the Joint Chiefs, to the Generals, to the Colonels, to the Captains and Lieutenants, to the Sergeants, and finally to the individuals. When the results start coming in, it starts from the bottom. First, a bridge is taken, then the buildings are cleared, the neighborhood is taken, the city is taken, the capital is taken, and the country has finally been conquered, right?" I explained in terms I knew she would understand.

"I get it now," she said.

"Everyone in the company will take their goal from the bigger goal you set. The next thing after that is to keep them accountable by setting metrics. What I like about setting clear metrics is that everyone would know the minimum, right? Some employees will do the bare minimum too. They'll only do the five percent growth you asked for and not an inch more. Tying a bonus to the level of growth they achieve will get you better results than what you expect. You can also tie the bonus to anything above the goal. If five percent is what is needed to grow the company, then the bonus may only be paid for results above the minimum. You also shouldn't be greedy. The more money they bring in for you, the more they should make. They worked for it so why not share some of that with them? If they don't make their target, hold the benefit back.

"Here's another example. If Jim already has his task but he chooses not to follow through, you could tell him, 'I want you to manage your relationship with this person.' He could reply, 'Yeah, I tried but it's too hard, so let's leave it.' Why should he apply himself completely to the task if there's no accountability? If you say, 'Well, you can bid goodbye to your quarterly bonus if that relationship is not properly managed' or, 'Sorry, but you won't get fully paid if you don't achieve results' then you might see some action. Some employees think it's enough to wear their suits and warm their seats throughout the day. It's not enough. If all they are doing is showing up without accomplishing anything, then they should not get any extra pay."

"Shouldn't I ask why they failed? You told me to always ask why," Liv recalled.

"Some targets can't be hit every quarter so let's say you do this every six months. You would ask Jim what is happening with the client that makes it difficult to satisfy them since he is responsible for the current customers. Ask why it is happening and go from there. The base reason could be that you're not keeping track of your customer's business too.

"Of course, your client's business is your business. Remember the story I told you earlier about the regulations surrounding underground gas tanks and how a lot of gas stations didn't do what they were supposed to? Thousands of gas stations went out of business overnight and a bunch of vendors who supplied products to the gas stations lost major streams of revenue. If the vendors had paid attention to the regulations that affected their clients, they would've known what was coming and been able to plan and pivot way before this happened.

"They were not working on their relationship with these customers. When the time came to replace the gas pumps most of the gas stations could not afford to. They had no choice but to stop pumping gas. They just had to lock the tanks. So, my client lost their best customer base just like that. Don't make that mistake. You need to know all the constraints your client's company has or at least know there could be issues coming.

"Look at Tom, that computer guy who introduced Steve to the new clients you now have. When you achieve your growth and hire more workers, who will you be buying the computers from?"

"Definitely Tom!" she said.

"Exactly. If he didn't keep a good relationship with Steve, he wouldn't have known you needed clients too. If you had to close shop, he would have lost a promising client too. Also, you should have smaller milestones to gain your growth. If you plan to grow a hundred percent but your milestone is at fifteen percent, you can give Jim five percent of that growth to achieve. I say fifteen percent because your goal needs to be realizable. Plus, if Jim does not achieve that, he will answer to you."

"Oh, and I hate confrontation," she said.

Confronting Uncomfortable Conversations

"Most people are not comfortable being the bad boss, but the success of the company starts and stops with you as the CEO. It is your name on the shingle. If your manager or an employee is underperforming, you need to address it quickly. Work through the "Five Whys" and find out what the problem is so you can try to address it. If it's a disciplinary thing, you should take care of it before it worsens. When you ignore confrontation because it's not in your nature, things will get worse. The employee may not even know how they are ruining things for the company. One day you won't be able to take it any longer and you'll have to fire them. There's nothing worse than the employee coming into your office as you wait for them, letter in hand, but you've done no constructive counseling in the past. It'll all come as a rude shock to them. They may even turn hostile by trying to ruin the reputation of your company. The worst part is that it'll all be your fault."

"How is it all your fault?" Liv asked.

"It's your fault for not giving them a chance to mend their ways. They don't know what your dream is for the company. You don't know their dreams either. If you had confronted them when the signs were just coming up, you could have noticed that they didn't like the department they were in, for example. You could have said, 'Hey, you're not a BD guy. Can we move you somewhere else?'

"This brings us to the apostle methodology we have discussed—where you help an off-ramped employee find a job somewhere else so that they can still be in a good relationship with you when they leave. They can then recommend you to their new employer.

"Your confrontation will be easier if you've set clear goals in the beginning. You will be able to call your managers in and ask, 'Steve, I gave you fifteen percent of that growth. Jim, I gave you five percent, but neither of you has achieved it. What's your plan? What is happening in the team?' Have them sit down with you and work through the plan. You may have a flaw in some parts of your strategy. This will also point to underperformance if that is the real issue, so that will be easier to spot and address.

"That's how you manage your relationship with your employees—not through confrontation, but through a discussion about failing to meet the goal. Your people should be able to know that they can come to you with any problem before it worsens. If they can easily approach you with any problem, it'll cut down on your confrontation. You may not like confrontation, but it is your responsibility to make sure the company is successful. This doesn't mean that you should be a hard boss either.

"Effective communication will help minimize confrontations—this topic deserves a more in-depth discussion at another time. However, I must stress the importance of setting metrics to avoid the conflicts that most of you detest, at least for as long as possible. Just as it happened when I confronted Steve, right? It was a challenging conversation, but we had it, and things have been running smoothly since in our story. That discussion brought to light some underlying issues that neither you nor Steve were fully aware of.

Setting Metrics For Lead Quality

"Liv, you still have some work to do with Steve and his team. He is doing better but you want to hold him accountable for everything he does in each quadrant. I've told you about figuring out your client's timetables.

"Whatever lead you're chasing needs to be achievable. If the lead is unrealistic, take it off the sheet because you don't need unpromising leads. You don't want Steve to have too many leads that he cannot chase. Some Managers will only have two people in their BD but will have 50 leads in their pipeline. Two people can't chase 50 leads. Unpromising leads should not clutter Steve's worksheet if he wants to achieve the target you set for him."

How do you think I should handle the bonus or compensation?" she asked.

"I've seen companies that do bonus pay by group. If Operations hit seven percent, which is higher than their five percent target, they will get a bigger bonus because they exceeded expectations. If the BD guys were supposed to get fifteen percent but they got fourteen or sixteen percent, you'll have to figure out how you want to plug the accountability and the reward by unit. Do you have any other questions?" I asked her.

"Yes. How do I differentiate between a promising lead and an unpromising one?"

"The key to holding them accountable is by having them take the lead to your accountability sheet for the MAN. You can create a sheet where all the leads your company is pursuing are documented. Whenever they bring you a lead, you should add it to the sheet. If Steve can't identify the MAN of their lead, there's a gap. Someone needs to figure that part out before the lead can be added to your accountability sheet."

"That will be my criteria for putting anything on the sheet," she stated.

"Yes," I agreed. "He's got to deliver the objective evidence that he knows that customer or that he can get to that customer. If he can't, that's an unpromising lead."

"If they need more time to find this MAN, how long can I give them?" she asked.

"Normally, when you're looking for new customers, two people need to be on the sheet within a month. If no one is added to the sheet within a month, then your team is not working on it the way they should be. During that time, they should have been able to figure out the MAN through the internet, phone calls, emails, and friends." I explained. "It's almost the end of this session and we have one final thing to talk about—the SMART process. I kept it for the last because you must have heard of it. After all, there are hundreds of books on SMART."

"Yes, I've heard about it," Liv confirmed.

Harnessing The Power Of Smart Goals In Building Strategic Relationships

"The SMART process isn't a new thing in business, but I want to tell you about it according to how you can use it to scale your relationship goals.

"SMART goals, as you know, means setting goals that are Simple, Measurable, Achievable, Realistic, and Timely. This means all of these should fit into your plan to find and build a relationship with the MAN. You should have a process for how you want to drill into different companies, although each one of your salespeople might apply that process a little differently.

"For instance, Julie might approach companies and reach out through social media, unlike Steve, who prefers physical interactions. Either approach is acceptable as long as they deliver results. There's nothing wrong with it as long as they follow your process. Once they establish the process, they will align their efforts with the company's goals.

"What impact will this SMART process have on our success?" Liv asked.

"It'll set the criteria for your success. As the CEO, your success can have broad implications. Your job isn't to build the plan to reach the customers; that's what your managers are for. If you're building the plan all the way down to the customer level, it might indicate that there are redundant managers in your organizational chart.

"Just because they are strategic partners doesn't mean you should divulge the entire plan to them. You don't have the bandwidth to be concerned with every single detail, such as every phone call they're going to make or every email they're going to send. You simply need to ensure that if, for example, you select Stall Mart as a strategic customer, they understand the significance and adhere to the process.

"When it comes to executing SMART every company is different, there is no one-size-fits-all all. You can execute yours by asking questions when you're setting your goals for relationship management and the MAN. You can ask your managers these questions. Ask them if the goal is Simple, Measurable, Achievable, Realistic and Timely. They should be able to answer 'Yes' to everything. If they say 'No' to any of those categories, then you need to ask the Five Whys. When you set these goals with your SMART process, there won't be any confusion between the employees, the Managers, and you. It'll be transparent all the way through."

"Do you have any questions before we close this session?" I asked as we both got up from our seats, signaling the end of our meeting.

Liv looked deep in thought. "It's not just about the SMART process, is it? It's about me holding the overarching vision and relying on my managers to handle the details while ensuring the SMART criteria are met. Am I on the right track?"

"Spot on," I affirmed, holding the door open for her. We began to walk down the hallway together, making our way to the exit. The soft hum of activity in other offices surrounded us. "But here's a thought: how often do you reckon you should revisit these goals?"

She glanced out the windows lining the hallway, watching the trees sway gently in the wind. "Quarterly reviews?"

"That's a start. Depending on the pace of your business, even monthly check-ins could be beneficial," I commented, leading the way to the parking lot where my Ford truck was parked.

She nodded, taking in the cool evening air. "So, in essence, these meetings either reinforce our direction or indicate where we need course correction."

"Exactly," I replied, pausing beside my truck. "Think of it like the 'blocking and tackling strategy' in football. Having star players is one thing, but if your frontline fails, the game's over. How does that resonate with your CEO role?"

Liv chuckled, leaning against the truck, her expression playful. "It means we can't just chase dreams; we need a solid foundation. It's about setting the right criteria, having clear goals, and tracking our achievements."

I unlocked the truck, smiling approvingly. "You've got it. Remember, Liv, without that foundation, it's like sidelining your best players."

She offered a firm handshake. "Thanks for the insights, Brian. I've got a lot to think about."

Watching her walk away, I felt confident in her journey ahead. A purposeful path was unfolding for Liv and her company, and with the right strategies in place, success was well within reach.

CHAPTER EIGHT

LEADING THE CHARGE: EFFECTIVE MANAGEMENT IN EXPANDING HORIZONS

"Good morning, Brian," Kerry greeted me as I walked into the company.

"Hey, Kerry," I said.

Liv, Steve, Jim and Susan were already waiting for me when I entered the conference room. I exchanged pleasantries, especially with Jim whom I hadn't seen for a couple of weeks.

When they settled in, I started. "Thank you, everyone. It's a pleasure to be here again. Liv has discussed what I told her during our last meeting with you, I hope?"

"Yes, she did," Jim answered. "The importance of relationship management, setting metrics, and accountability?"

"Perfect. So, today, we will continue with the subject of accountability. First, we will discuss how Liv can hold Steve accountable for his department," I said.

"If I didn't know any better, Brian, I would say you're picking on my department," Steve joked.

"Well, the bulk of the work is on you so maybe I am," I said with a laugh. "It's the job you signed up for. I'll still talk about Operations too."

Defining Accountability with MAN and Quadrants

"So, Steve, we talked about finding the MAN in your target, right? I want to remind everybody, and Jim who wasn't here when we talked about it, that as we put information into the quadrants, we want to find out who has control in the company we're trying to make our client, so that we can build relationships with the MAN. Now let's look at the updated Quadrants charts?"

Opportunity Matrix			
Quadrant		Quadrant	
I. Existing Customer/ Existing Capability **(5%)**	• XYZ Inc. (DA) • International Inc. (BI)	III. New Customer/ Existing Capability **(45%)**	• Humana (DA) • Tricore (BI) • ACME Testing (Enhanced DA)
II. Existing Customer/ New Capability **(40%)**	XYZ Inc. (Enhanced DA)	IV. New Customer/ New Capability **(10%)**	• Beneficial Govt (Enhanced BI) • Stalmart (Enhanced

Fig. Accountability In The Four Quadrants

"Those are the four quadrants and the percentage of growth Liv wants you to achieve in each quadrant. These percentages will keep you accountable for how you contribute to the growth of this company. Now, these percentages are also going to be our first attempt at trying to implement an accountability plan. If you think we're off base with this, let us know."

Steve looked up and asked, "Me?"

"Your input is important to the plan, Steve. You're the leader of this company's foot soldiers. Is the percentage in each quadrant achievable?" I asked again.

"Let me see," he looked at the chart again.

I started to lead them through it. "I spoke with Liv and we decided to plan a five percent growth in quadrant one; existing customers on existing capability."

"My team can get behind that," Steve confirmed.

"Awesome," I commended. "In quadrant two, we planned for forty percent growth. As you can see, XYZ Inc. is an existing customer with this company but they are only buying Data Analysis from you. Since you now have a new enhanced data analysis product, thanks to Jim and his team, is there a way you can sell the new product to XYZ? Liv believes that we can create a forty percent growth there. Based on the capability of your team and the relationship you currently have there, do you think that is achievable?"

Steve looked at Liv for permission and she nodded.

"Okay. That one is not realistic," he said. "We don't have that type of relationship with them yet. Can I come back to you and Liv after doing some analysis on that one? We might need to bring another company into quadrant two if the goal is to achieve forty percent."

"That makes sense," I agreed. "Now, in quadrant three, you see we're at forty-five percent. Quadrant four, ten percent. In other words, we want to swing for some home runs, but we don't want it to be half the business development. What I want from you now, Steve, is for you to take these percentages, go back to your MAN chart in each company you are currently building a relationship with, and start breaking these percentages down for your people. After that, I need you to bring your result back to Liv so that we can talk about it."

"I think I understand the way you're trying to do the percentages," Steve replied. "My team will look at it."

"I'm sure you're already looking at it. I've heard of the incredible results you've achieved. I just want you to digest it again. Focus on the goal, right? Can you get back to Liv in three days?"

Steve thought hard and finally answered, "Four days."

I looked at Liv and asked, "Is that good for you, Liv?"

"Yes," she answered.

"Okay, because we need to establish this accountability to chart our way forward. We can't proceed without setting our house in order, can we? Your team, Steve, needs to grasp the significance of the assigned percentages. Their percentages will aggregate to your department's, which will then accumulate to Liv's. They must comprehend their precise roles in each quadrant."

"Okay, Brian. I'll make sure they understand," Steve said.

"I want to emphasize the importance of new customer acquisition for expansion. As you can see, this quadrant will account for forty-five percent—in the third quadrant—and ten percent growth in the fourth quadrant, which means new customers are needed for the company's fifty-five percent growth. We weighted it heavier on existing capability so that everything is not brand new. I also want to utilize the MAN charts for lead accountability."

"How?" Jim asked.

"Every time Steve reports to Liv about any lead his department is chasing, he has to provide the MAN chart for each lead."

"What does that chart look like?" Steve asked.

I pulled one out of my backpack and showed them.

Who is the MAN?				
Key Customers Decision Makers				
Organization	**Lead**	**Money (M)**	**Authority (A)**	**Need (N) End User**
XYZ Inc.	Steve	John	Sam	Ben
Key Stakeholders				
Key Decision	**Issue/ Hot Button/ Need**	**Weight (1-10)**		
	International Inc.			
		Humana		
			Tricore	

If he is chasing eight leads, each lead should have eight MAN charts. Then Liv will build from that to figure out where you're at with the communications plan for your opportunity. How are you meeting the key influencers in the MAN chart? How are you building your relationship with them? By creating the MAN chart for each lead, Liv will be able to better keep an eye on you."

"I've got it," Steve said. "I'll work with my team to make sure we get the numbers right and then lay out our communications plan on where I think our holes are."

"Do you understand what I mean by the MAN chart for each lead?" I inquired.

"Yes, I do. There will be a MAN chart for XYZ Inc., another MAN chart for Humana Tracker, and so on."

"That's right," I said.

"Let me restate, the four quadrants and their percentages only work if those on board truly understand how to get to the percentages and how they hold you accountable. It is a formula that will hold true no matter who the client or customer is or that you currently have or hope to have in the future. The MAN and Four Quadrants work in any industry."

Contract Kickoff Meeting: Bridging Sales to Operations

"So, Jim,I said that your department was the next I would talk to about relationship management and accountability. I could have talked to you alone but the Program Managers are important to your department. They are here because they need to know what will be expected from now on.

"You'll all be aware," I said, directing my attention back to the whole room, "that this company has undergone some changes in the past few months. Now, this change has reached you. It won't be easy but I, and Liv, expect you to accept these changes. This is not only for the sake of the company as a whole but to make your work easier. Are we on the same page?"

"Good. I've spoken with Business Development about their role in the company and how they will be held accountable for every lead they chase from now on. So, we've come to the roles of the Department of Operations and how we can hold you accountable for how you carry it out."

"Where does our role start then?" Jim asked.

"At the handoff. It's when Steve's department brings you a deal. They've done their job by winning a client for the company. The next thing is for them to hand this client to you, Since you're the one who will supply whatever service or products the client wants to buy. But there are processes as well.

"The first thing is a contract kickoff meeting. It's pretty straightforward. The meeting is meant to cover all the actions the company will take before we officially recognize a lead as a client. For example, Steve brings you a lead from XYZ. Before it reaches your table, he has worked on his relationship with the company. When he hands the deal to your department, the relationship management still has to continue. Your department needs to start asking some questions once you've been handed the deal."

"What questions?" Jim asked.

"Questions like, 'Has the client sent an official proposal to us?', 'Has all the data the client told Steve been sent to the Contract Department—or whoever handles your contract?', 'Has that same data been sent to the Finance Department and the Manager of the Operations Department?' It's important to send a copy of the data to all these departments to make sure that the data is properly reviewed to avoid discrepancies. The one thing we don't want to do is deliver blue shoes to a client who asked for black shoes or give a Data Analysis package to the client who asked for Business

Intelligence. It's during this meeting that you need to ask all these questions. Who is your Contract Reviewer?"

"She's not here," Anne said.

"But you have someone who is good at the job?"

"Yes. She's good. I can attest to that," Steve said.

"Awesome. Then the job of the Contract Reviewer, as you know, is to make sure the contract is fully executed as the client specified. They will take a look at all the data to make sure they have what the company needs to load the contract into the system. When the reviewer and the other departments are done reviewing the draft, they will pass it to Jim because he needs to know what the Operations Department is contractually held to. This contract is what Liv will hold the entire Operations Department up to."

"This contract kickoff meeting is what gives birth to the contract kickoff table. "Please take a look at the table labeled 'Contract Kickoff Table'.

COMPANY		Contract Kickoff Checklist	
Date:			
Attendees:			
Contract Identifier-Internal			
Contract No.			
Action	Notes	Owner	Completion date
Proposal sent to Contracts		Business Unit Lead	
Contracts			
Contract checked against proposal submitted for discrepancies		Business Unit Lead/ Contracts	
Contract Fully Executed		Contracts	
Contract information communicated to Finance for Accounting Setup		Contracts	
Labor Categories and bill rates		Contracts	
Travel allowed?		Contracts	
Materials?		Contracts	
Invoicing details		Contracts	
Reporting/deliverable requirements communicated to assigned PM		Contracts	
Are there any Security requirements?		Contracts	
Subcontracts Required		Contracts	
Send RFP to potential subcontractors		Contracts	
Evaluate RFP responses for compliance with Customer Contract		Contracts	
Review evaluations with Operations Team		Contracts/ PM	
Operations			
Program Manager Assigned		Business Unit Lead	
Personnel Identified		Program Manager	

Personnel qualifications confirmed prior to assignments being sent to Finance		Program Manager	
Personnel assignments sent to Finance		Program Manager	
If not, job requisition needs to be submitted to HR		Program Manager	
Program meeting scheduled to review SOW with assigned personnel		Program Manager	
Review project budget prior to input into finance system		Kick Off Team	
Submit project budget to Finance			
***Subcontracts required?**		Business Unit Lead/ PM	
Provide RFP to contracts to send to subcontractor		Program Manager	
Submit subcontractor POC info to contracts		Program Manager	
Submit subcontractor SOW to contracts		Program Manager	
Finance			
Set up project in project in the Finance System		Finance	
Complete personnel assignments in system		Finance	
Input project budget into system		Project Controller	
HR			
HR to begin recruiting		HR	
Resume review		PM/HR	
Interviews		PM/HR	
Coordination of contract specific training (certifications, program specific or DoD)	Ex/ Special tool equipment operation, IT, etc.		

Logistics/IT			
Equipment needed	*costs require approval if not built into annual operating budget		
Office space needed			
Additional requirements			

Fig. Contract Kickoff Table

The Critical Role of Program Managers in Bridging the Gap Between Promise and Delivery

"Jim, look at this table closely, you'll see that under the operations section it talks about your Program Managers, Anne and Peter. This means that you need to assign them to oversee that deal as soon as Steve hands it to you. This needs to be done before the contract kickoff meeting really. The Program Manager is who Jim will hold accountable for that client. Before you sign off and hand the deal to them, you also need to make sure they have everything they need to be successful. After that, you task the PM and give them the project's responsibilities. Any questions, Jim?" I asked.

"None for now," he replied.

"This brings us to the role of the Program Managers. So that you can understand the importance of your position, you should know Steve and his team worked extremely hard to bring a lead to your table. They could have worked for months to build the relationship that eventually landed that deal. If you do not do your job properly, you could jeopardize all that work."

Anne and Peter shifted uncomfortably in their seats then became more attentive.

"Above all else, the client expects flawless delivery of their service or product. Any errors on our part could compromise our relationship with the client and damage their expectations."

"Right," Anne said.

"So, as the Program Managers, you need to read the statements of work as soon as you're assigned a project. If there's an issue where you need subcontractors, vendors, or any other type of support, you need to identify these issues during the contract kickoff meeting."

"Is that meeting for the entire company or just the Operations Department?" Steve asked.

"Yes. It's for everyone who will have a copy of the client's data, as I mentioned earlier. That's the Finance Department, the Contract Reviewer, the Program Managers, and the Operations Manager. When you hold the contract kickoff meeting, everyone needs to know which parts of the deal will be outsourced. There should be information on any missing costs that a certain department could have missed. When you walk out of that meeting, everybody should have what they need."

“Are there other things expected from us?” Peter asked.

“You will coordinate with the Finance Manager to make sure that the Finance Department knows what you need. This means you will set up charge codes, billing, travel costs, or any other bills related to that deal. Does that make sense?”

“Yes it does make sense,” Peter said. “We’ve been doing a version of that.”

“Good. After you’ve analyzed that deal, you should know if you have the necessary skills to finish the job or if you need more help. If you need more help, you can go to Jim and he’ll ensure the necessary positions are hired as soon as possible. You should consider how fast you can conduct interviews to start hiring too.”

“All these rest on proper communication and good relationship management,” Jim noted.

“Yes, it does. The last thing you need to consider as soon as you’re handed the project is logistics. Does everybody need laptops? Are there things that need to be purchased to set the program up?”

“Brian, I think I’ve got it. I’ve been looking at the contract kickoff table that you shared with us. It does a great job. We can use this as the outline for our future tasks. Maybe we’ll add some additional pieces to it,” Steve said.

"Great. As for the Program Managers, you need to attend this contract kickoff meeting too. Since you've gone through the contract outline, you need to make sure that the sales guys did not overpromise on what you can deliver. You know these Business Development guys do it all the time."

Anne and Peter shared a knowing look and laughed.

"Sales guys can say a lot of things to sell something to the customer. They can say, 'Hey, don't worry. We can fix all your data analysis worries within ten days. Do you want it in five? Sure, we can do that too.' But then you look at the table, read the outline and go, 'No, we can't do that.' When something like this happens, it is important to catch it as soon as possible. Then you can tell the salesperson who overpromised, 'No, that can't happen. It'll cost us more money and there's no way we'll get the money to pay for that.' So, a contract kickoff meeting is not just a formality. When you show up, you should be ready to play ball and understand what your lane is. When you're done, everyone should have understood their responsibilities. This is called operational accountability. When you've understood what you're supposed to do, you will be held accountable if you do not do it."

Rewarding Growth Over Mediocrity

"How do I enforce this accountability for my department?" Jim asked.

"You can start by setting up a bonus structure for every success your team achieves. You can collaborate with Liv on this. She understands the importance of setting a base standard for the performance of everyone in the company. For instance, Liv might tie Jim and his Program Managers' bonuses to the growth of their program. She could say, 'If you guys don't grow your program by five percent, you don't get a bonus.' In other words, she pays you to manage your programs. If you want anything extra in your pay you have to help the company grow. That's what I recommended that Liv should do with the Business Development department, and it's what I'll recommend she do with the Operations department too. Jim, you can take a cue from that and apply it to the workers in your department."

Jim raised his hand. "I'm just confused about the five percent growth you were talking about," he said.

"Okay. Look at it this way. Let's say your program is worth $1 million this year. If by this time next year, you haven't grown the program to at least $1 million and $50,000, then you haven't achieved any growth. Whatever Liv pays you is for doing your job. You don't deserve any bonus for that. However, if you grow your program, you should be rewarded for that, no matter how modest the compensation will be. Any bonuses should be tied to growth."

"Got it," Jim agreed.

I turned to Liv who had been listening intently to everything we were saying, "CEOs should be rewarding growth, not mediocrity. This is business, not a children's sport where everyone gets a participation trophy," I said.

"Yes," Liv Said, "I want the company focused and growing. Which is why I am behind this model to take care of those taking care of the company."

"I think I understand you now," Jim said.

"What do you understand?" I questioned, feeling like maybe he didn't get it.

"I need to set targets for my team. If they don't meet them, they don't get a bonus."

"No, that's not what I was saying." I paused. "If they don't meet the target, we might replace them. If they don't *exceed* the goal, they don't get a bonus. There's a difference and you need to tell them that difference clearly so that there'll be no discrepancy. The amount you'll pay them for the bonus doesn't matter. It could be $500 or $20,000."

"It's not uncommon for this to get confusing. However, this confusion can also lead to disgruntled employees. Communication and knowing the expectation is so important for everyone to be on the same page.

"What's important is that you pay for project growth, not just for them to show up and go to work. Any other questions?" I looked around the room, but no one showed any sign of needing to ask further questions.

Strategies for Expansion

"Since we're on the subject of growth, I've been thinking about your goal of expansion. Liv, there have been discussions about your dream of taking your business to Europe, I believe."

"Yes," she replied, "I'm looking towards Europe for our expansion after we've firmly set our roots in the US."

"Where would you start in Europe?" I questioned.

"Germany," Liv answered without hesitation. "I know a little about the country because I served there. I'm also thinking about England. The prospects there are good."

"Okay, I can understand that. How do you see that goal happening in your mind?" I asked.

"I'm still rolling it around in there," she said as she pointed to her head.

"There are several factors and strategies for expansion," I said.

Factors to Consider for an Effective Expansion Strategy

"You can develop one by playing to your company's strength. We want to have a higher percentage of work and a higher probability of winning areas, right? So, we want to stay in those quadrants where we know we can win. If you already have customers in the new area, thanks to your consultant, then you should focus on quadrants one and two. If you don't have existing customers but you have a good track record in your capability, then you should enter the market with a strategy built around the third quadrant. What you should avoid is a new, new situation."

"What's a new, new situation?" Liv asked.

"When you don't have existing customers in the market you're expanding to, and you are also not an expert in the service or product you're selling."

"That makes sense," Liv said.

"Not only does the strategy need to fit the company's strength, but it also needs to be tailored around the team's strength. Some of your workers will be good at dealing with new customers while others are better at dealing with existing ones. Expansion, after all, is also dependent on relationship management.

"Let's take a moment to discuss consultants," I said.

"Well, Steve and I have been trying to decide when the right time to hire someone is. Do we have to hire a person in the country?" Liv asked.

"I assume you've been contemplating hiring a consultant in the target country for your expansion," I said. "My suggestion is to identify a reliable in-country consultant who can be held accountable by Steve or one of his team members in Business Development. This ensures that the consultant remains aligned with the company's goals. But before we delve deeper, let's consider some key factors.

"If you don't have a good relationship with the clients your consultant found for you, it'll be hard for you to keep a strong base in that market. If your strategy for expansion is to acquire new clients, then you should send someone who knows how to talk to new clients. Every member of your team is unique."

"True," Peter agreed.

"At least we know some people are better closers than the others," I said. "Since we're considering personalities, we should consider execution too. In this case, some people can tee up the deal, but we need to bring a closer to finish the deal. If your consultant is good at bringing in clients, for instance, Steve could be your company's lead who holds the consultant accountable. That way, most of the deals can be finished. The aim is to show the customer how this company works as a team to solve all their problems. When you show clients how capable you are, the next thing you know you're a national company trying to go international.

Local Consultants in Expansion

"Do you have any questions about consultants?" I asked.

"Are we supposed to treat them like they are employees?" Liv questioned.

"You could decide to retain the consultant in that branch after their work is done or you only work with them until they've helped you create a presence in Europe. In response to your question, Liv, you will treat them like they are one of your employees. Their role needs to be well defined, like that of everyone sitting around this table. You need to decide how you will pay them, will it be weekly, monthly, or according to the tasks they complete? How will you incentivize them when they achieve beyond the goals you set them? You also need to consider if they are good relationship managers. Incorporating these questions into your expansion strategy will be crucial."

Remote Research vs. Onsite Research

"The next thing you need to consider is how much research you can conduct remotely about the expansion location. You can't just jump blindly into a market you don't know. A part of your strategy involves determining how you will research the market you're entering. If Steve is chosen as the lead that the consultant reports to, for example, he will need a detailed list of the work he wants the consultant to do, similar to a scope of work. What do you need to know? Every market should be approached with this level of structure, whether it's regional, national, or international. You need to ensure you have a structured approach to enter the market and sustain any growth you achieve in it."

"How do we know when we're ready to start this expansion?" Steve asked.

"There's no physical line for you to cross if that's what you mean. There's no exact dollar figure that you need to have before you start considering expansion. It's a decision you and Liv will have to make based on a risk model. It also depends on when you believe you're ready to put somebody in that country full time," I said.

"Is that not why we have the consultant?" Liv inquired.

"Yes, but what happens if the consultant becomes extremely successful? If they are gently working as you are on a growth trajectory, things will be easy for you because the consultant can handle it. Things will become complicated if the consultant achieves the growth faster than you predicted and they suddenly can't keep up with it," I responded.

"What happens then?" asked Anne.

"Then you have to evaluate the situation by committing company funds and getting someone there faster so that they can assist the consultant."

Embracing Regional Legal and Cultural Differences

"We've been talking about the company and the team," Steve noted. "What about the customer? Surely we need to consider them in the strategy too."

"You're absolutely right," I answered. "One of the ways you can consider the client is by adapting regional differences to your strategy. Even within the US, there are different areas of the country, the Southeast, Northwest, and so on. These areas have different buying patterns. They have different accents, even though we all speak English. As we're building a relationship with our clients in other parts of the country or other parts of the world, you need to pay attention to cultural differences. An example could be how clients prefer to be greeted. Some people shake hands, some fist bump, while others like a hug. You need to keep in touch with what's accepted in different cultures and what's not. You don't want to turn potential clients off because you acted in a way that is considered culturally unacceptable or you used a word that meant an entirely different thing in that region.

"That's where the consultant comes in again. They are local, so they know the things that their culture doesn't allow. This knowledge about regional differences is not limited to clients alone. You should teach them to properly relate with employees on that side of the world too, if you eventually hire some. Any questions?"

There were none, but I could see this was a lot to digest.

Regional Customs and Laws

"The last thing we have to cover today is the legal framework of the place we're expanding to. In the United States alone, every state and county has its own set of laws that may be different from the laws of other states. What is legal in New York may not be legal in Florida. When we go to England or Germany, their ways are different as well. There will be laws that we're not used to in the US. Let's make sure it's part of your risk management and Business Development to look at the laws and the customs. I know this sounds crazy but think about things like: Are there colors we can't use there? Are there words we can't say? Don't send a red banner to a country that doesn't like red. Maybe they want everything to be green, blue, or white. It's very important to know those laws and customs.

"Imagine you're invited to the funeral ceremony of a potential client's grandparents, and you show up in a black suit, not knowing that the mourning color of that country is white. Then you embarrass yourself because you're the only odd person there. Not to mention that it's an awkward start to the relationship with that prospective client. Ignorance can cost you more than that. In fact, it's better to just hire a lawyer in that country before you move in. They will guide you into avoiding business laws that may end up ruining your ambition or your ability to work in that place."

As the discussion drew to a close, my alarm went off, signaling the end of our meeting. "Liv, can you wait a minute, please?" I asked, looking at her expectantly.

"Sure," she replied, taking a seat.

"How do you feel that went?" I asked her.

"There's a lot of details that we've managed to work out and our process is getting better. As long as we continue to implement the lessons we learn from you, we will continue to improve," she said.

"Awesome. Just don't forget that we're all here because of your vision. It's why you hired me and it's why you hired everyone that just left this room. Next week, I want these same people in the room for our next discussion. Is that possible?"

"Anything you need, Brian," she confirmed.

CHAPTER NINE
COMMUNICATION, CONTRACT AND CONFLICTS:
BUILDING AND MANAGING CLIENT RELATIONSHIPS

As Steve entered the conference room, he greeted me with a warm handshake. It had only been a week since our last meeting, but I was excited to talk to the team about how relationships and communication are at the heart of success in business. I knew that these were two essential pillars that every entrepreneur, manager, and team leader needed to master.

"How's work coming along?" I asked, breaking the ice.

Steve replied, "It's moving, so I can't complain." He settled into his seat, his notes and iPad in tow, as he shed his jacket.

"A friend is hosting a relationship management conference next week," I revealed, "and I'd like you to be there."

“To be where?” Liv asked as she walked into the room.

“I was telling Steve about a conference I want him to join next week—BIMC,” I said.

The title alone left them momentarily dumbfounded. Their astonishment soon gave way to excitement.

“Get out of here!” Liv exclaimed. “That is the most exclusive conference in this part of Florida. How do you expect us to get in?”

With a chuckle, I unveiled two tickets. “Luckily for us, I know someone who knows someone. Conferences are essential, right? A lot of business dealings and connections happen there but most importantly, you meet people, and they meet you. Are you interested?”

Steve wasted no time seizing one of the tickets, and Liv, still in disbelief, accepted the other. Gratitude filled the room as she finally said, “Thank you.”

“You're welcome. Conferences are a great way to meet like-minded people and promote your company. I attend a bunch each year to stay in the loop and connect with clients. When you go the extra mile to chat with clients about their industry, it really impresses them. I remember once I went to a client's industry conference, and they were thrilled I showed up. The $1000 I spent on the ticket was nothing compared to the contract I secured.

"At these events, it's all about making connections and looking ahead. Steve, you'll need to figure out who your potential clients are and plan some face-to-face time with them. I usually do some research beforehand, making a list of people I want to meet. Sometimes, I even book future meetings right there at the conference, so we can get down to business. And hey, what better way to do that than over a nice lunch?"

"I can't wait!" Steve said.

"And Liv?" I asked, turning to face her. "I'd love to meet up with Susan again after the conference to discuss the Finance department. Can you make that happen?"

"Yes, absolutely, I can." she said emphatically.

When Jim and his two program managers joined the meeting and took their seats, we shifted gears back to our core agenda.

Building Trust With Your Client Through Communication

"Welcome back everyone," I started. "You're looking sharp, Anne. So, we're still talking about how to properly manage relationships with the client. Tell me, Steve, what is the basis of every relationship?"

"Trust?" Steve replied.

"Yes, but that one is earned. What facilitates it?" I asked.

"Communication," Anne offered.

I could tell our work was paying off, they were all on the same page. "Yes, it's all about talking and listening. From the very start, we need to be on the same page with our customers. It's like building a good relationship with a new neighbor. You want to know what they're up to, and they want to know about you too. This communication thing doesn't just stop with Steve's team; even Jim's got a role to play with the higher-ups in the client company. We want this relationship to run smoothly, from the guys on the ground all the way up the ladder."

"The big shots, right?" Liv asked.

"Exactly," I confirmed. "We want to create an environment where clients can give us the lowdown without any fuss. If they're facing any hiccups with our process, we want them to tell us as soon as they detect it. If there's some new rule that might throw them off, we need to be the first to fill them in. That's the trust we're after. Their criticism will make us more successful. We make more money, they make more money, and everyone is happy. That's the secret sauce for customer satisfaction."

Pushing forward, I added, "And it's not just about dealing with local rules. Imagine we're dealing with laws from two different states. We've got to make sure we all know how these rules might affect our game. If we're sending stuff across the border, we gotta figure out who's handling the taxes. Who's doing what role? We need a crystal-clear picture so we don't end up in a shouting match over something silly like, 'Hey, did your delivery guy drop off the goods?' 'What goods? I thought you were taking care of it!' You get the drift. You can imagine how disastrous that would be to a relationship."

"Especially if it's a budding one," Steve said.

Policy Management

"There's also the matter of policy management. In every relationship you manage, there will always be external stakeholders. We can't control everything, right? The external stakeholders could be a list of stringent county, state, or federal laws and policies that we need to familiarize ourselves with. There'll be strange laws on their side and strange laws on our side. What we need to do is not only learn about their side but our side as well. They could have skipped a rule somewhere. It'll then rest on us to say, 'Hey, I don't think we can do that. Our country does not allow it.' That's how we can avert a potential disaster," I said.

"But policies change, don't they?" Jim asked.

"They do, and that's why we're supposed to stay on top of trends. When a new policy that may impact our business or our client's business is made, we should know about it. I told you about the restaurants that didn't tell their gas clients about the government's policy of changing containers."

"Yeah," Liv confirmed.

"Don't be like them. We need to learn these policies so that we can know how to adapt to them and to customers who are not tracking them. We need a relationship where we can tell them, 'I heard about such and such policy. How will it affect you? Are there any adjustments we can make to help you through this?' In short, care about your client's business and show them that you care.

"Understanding comes before caring. So, understand your clients. We have to stay abreast of what our target clients are putting out. How are they buying? What is in their press releases? How do we interface with them? When you know and understand the prospective client, there won't be a need to pitch very often because the company would have already known what the client will warmly receive and what they are bound to ignore. Pitch less, win more. Any questions?" I asked.

"I have one," Jim answered. "How do we deal with introverts on the client's side? You also know that some people just want to sit in their cubicles and do their work. Yet, they are among the MAN or part of our key influencers. A relationship runs both ways, so how do we keep in contact with them?"

"Good question," I responded. "Introverts still have a voice and two ears." Everyone laughed. "They may not be the vocal ones in a sales meeting or an operations meeting, but we can talk to them, and they can talk back. You could still get them to feed you information on the quality of work your company is providing, the delivery quality, and other kinds of data. You just gather the data and run with it.

Communication

"The need for effective communication also extends to contracts. It's the key to meeting your client's expectations. You've been in business a while, Liv, so you're aware that clients often overlook certain mistakes if their requirements are met, although avoiding errors altogether is the best practice.

"A contract signifies your commitment to a client, and it's crucial to honor that commitment. This is why contracts should be meticulously reviewed. Before the Contract Reviewer or Contract Manager signs off on it, Steve and Jim need to review it thoroughly. Your Program Managers should also carefully scrutinize it. You must ensure that you can fulfill everything outlined in the document.

"There should be no under-the-table agreements, no informal arrangements, no concealed understandings. A single misstep could lead to losing control, accountability, and ultimately, the customer relationship, as you find ourselves at odds with the client over deliverables," I explained.

I paused to read the room. I still had my audience's undivided attention. Good. That was a lot to digest.

"This need for perfection, or something close to it, in our relationship management with clients means there has to be significant human involvement in contract relationships.

Relationship Management Honoring Commitments: The Interplay of Contracts and Relationship Management

"Since there's human interaction, there is a relationship that needs to be managed too. This time, I'm referring to communication within the company. If there is an issue with the original contract, then the person who has the best relationship with the customer should meet them to fix the issues before signing. If there's a place where the sales team over-promised, it needs to be identified unless the customer agrees to pay the extra cost that the additional feature would cause.

"The Program Managers," I continued, "need to keep a proper relationship with whoever is handling contract management. When you find problems, there needs to be an immediate conversation between the Operations department and the Contracts department to figure out how best to proceed. There can be no discrepancies internally in our capability. If the Contract Manager has some insights into the way the contract was written, there should be a proper communication channel for them to talk to the operations team and whoever is working on the project. Do you have any questions?" I asked.

The room was silent.

"As you care for your clients, you should also care for your employees. I'm not referring to Liv alone. Everyone here is a manager. This means you have people under your care. It's important to effectively manage these relationships too, through proper communication. You've heard of love languages, right? How do you embrace or talk to your employees and the co-workers in your care? Do you have a sound relationship with your employees that will enable you to figure out their love language? That's not rhetorical, Liv. Do you have a plan for it?"

"Oh," Liv said and chuckled. "Sorry. Yes, we are working on a plan for that. I've been reading *The Dream Manager* and I've learned the importance of paying attention to the employees' desires and dreams. I delegated that task to Jim."

"I should have a plan for you in the next three to four weeks," Jim jumped in.

"What's holding you up?" I inquired.

"Setting this up requires some investment. My team needs to gather all of the data to figure out that cost so that Liv can sign off on it. My PMs are already trying to cultivate a positive relationship with the other employees after your session with us last week," Jim submitted, but I wasn't satisfied yet.

"How are they trying to cultivate this relationship?" I asked.

"We had a meeting and for now, we've decided to do it through training. We 've noticed that there are some tools we're using that some of the employees don't know how to use. Since we've had a lot of work recently, they could not practice these tools at work. Instead, they practiced alone at home while feeling stuck in the office. We identified these tools and we decided to get the employees extra training..."

"How did you find out about this problem?"

"We asked them, like Liv told us to. We bought a suggestion box for the office and encouraged everyone to put in their problems. We even suggested they do it anonymously. Many of them mentioned inadequate training."

"How are you solving it now?"

"We hired someone from the local community college to teach them about the tools. We paid for five employees to attend a conference about the tools too."

"What was their reaction to it?" I asked.

"We've had positive feedback. They are happy because they know we're making sure they stay educated in an industry that is always evolving. They now understand where the market is going, which makes them feel more confident in their jobs. It also benefits the company because the training makes them faster and the results are better."

"This is brilliant!" I commented.

"Thank you," said Jim.

"I can see you have that handled so let's go back to communications. How are you handling relationship management in the crosstalk between your departments?"

"What?" Steve asked.

Mastering Crosstalk for Cohesive Collaborations

"A company is supposed to be a well-oiled machine; every cog, wheel, and bolt is supposed to work together without friction. Crosstalk is the oil that keeps everything frictionless. It's how you communicate the client's need to Jim and how these things are repeated to other departments so that they can make sure Jim follows that specification. The contract kickoff meeting, for instance, is another example of crosstalk. It allows everyone in the company to sit together, make corrections, and agree on issues, right?

"Crosstalk between the heads of Operations, Finance, Business Development, and Liv is the lifeblood of this company. There will be conflicts and confrontations, but they all need to be resolved at the management level. When crosstalk is properly done, discrepancies and needed changes will be dealt with faster."

"Conflicts in what way?" Jim questioned.

"Conflicts of interest. It happens all the time. Disagreements can happen within a company, but they should be kept right there—within the company. Clients should not learn about these conflicts. We don't want any issues with our customers or any of our vendors where there could be anything that looks like conflict" I explained.

"We will start training about crosstalk and how to solve this conflict of interest, right Jim?" Liv asked.

"I've made a note of that," Jim confirmed.

"Good. The key to conflict resolution is for the leadership to make sure the employees know how to report every conflict of interest before it jeopardizes your contract with the client. Steve, do you have a process for resolving these conflicts within the sales team?" I asked.

"We have a process in place," Steve answered with very little confidence, "but it's not very comprehensive yet. I've always made sure my co-workers can come to me with any of their grievances. We don't want to run into an issue with a customer."

"How about I give you some homework? Find a process that will include gratuities or gifts for coworkers who facilitate crosstalks in your department. Are we good with that?" I asked.

"Yeah, I'll work on it," he said.

"Great, then it looks like we're done for today," I said.

"That was a quick session," Liv commented.

I nodded, "Yes, it was. By the way, do you remember I mentioned I'll be meeting you, Steve, and Susan, your Finance Manager, at that conference?"

"Yes, I remember," Liv confirmed.

"It will be a great event and a chance for the team to use the Relationship Management techniques we have been talking about to open new doors for the team," said Steve. "I'm really looking forward to it."

I stood up, slightly stretching my back. "Well, it's been a productive day. I trust everyone will give these matters the attention they deserve. Liv, Steve, Susan—I would look forward to seeing you at the conference."

There were nods around the table. As chairs began to push back and papers shuffled, Liv approached me, "Brian let me walk you out," she offered.

"Thank you, Liv." We made our way through the office and the building. I opened the door for her, and we walked outside.

"You've given us so much to reflect on, I really appreciate the direction you're giving us."

I gave her a reassuring smile, "It's a journey, Liv. I have confidence in your team. They're eager to adapt and that's half the battle."

She nodded, "Drive safe, Brian and thank you!" she said as I got into my truck. We waved good-bye and I drove home.

As I drove home that evening, I felt like we had a great day.

CHAPTER TEN
INVESTMENT INTIMACIES:
NURTURING RELATIONSHIPS FOR BUSINESS GROWTH

The next time I met Liv was at the business management conference I had invited her to. Josh, one of the primary coordinators of the conference, was a friend I met through one of my clients. He had attempted to sell me a property when we met. I did not buy that house but I recommended someone who did. We had grown close since that time. I met Todd, the man who introduced Liv and I, through Josh. Annually, he would organize a huge conference that a lot of movers and shakers would attend. He did not charge a lot of money for registration but getting an invitation to the event itself could be extremely hard. Therefore, it was not easy convincing him to give me three tickets for me, Steve, and Liv. He eventually relented when I promised to introduce him to a potential client.

On the day of the conference, I arrived earlier than the other guests to help Josh set up the conference hall. That was another condition of the tickets I got.

"You make me want to be one of your clients, Brian," Josh teased.

"Why is that?"

"The lengths you would go to look after their interest amazes me."

I just shrugged and continued to direct the young man to arrange the chairs like I was doing.

"Who do you want me to introduce them to?"

I looked at him in surprise when he asked that.

"What? You drew the short straw with the deal we made and you know it," he laughed, "I should at least help out however I can."

"Oh please. You just want to pitch your new idea to them," I countered and smiled.

He raised his hand in mock surrender, "Okay, you got me, but I still want to meet them. I'll pitch to them, they will pitch to me. In the end, everyone is happy."

"Fine. I'd like you to introduce them to Moses—the keynote speaker—and Victor."

Josh kept his promise after the conference ended. I watched as Steve spoke with Victor, CEO of a data analysis tool developer , who kept nodding in agreement.

"Hey, Brian? Are you listening?" Liv asked.

I snapped out of my train of thought and faced Liv, who had been talking to me while I was busy watching Steve and Victor.

"Sorry, Liv. What were you saying?"

"I asked where we could talk. Susan just called to say she's in the hotel's restaurant."

"Awesome. Let's go meet her."

She followed me as I stood up and made for the door. Before leaving, I turned to Steve and discreetly gave him a thumbs up. He returned it, still engaging his newfound friend.

Liv and I found Susan sitting in a corner of the restaurant, laptop out, typing away, a pot of fancy looking tea getting cold beside her. We made our way through the restaurant filled with business owners pitching their ideas to potential clients and eventually arrived at Susan's table.

"Hi, Brian," Susan greeted, "It's nice to see you. I am thrilled to get to work with you at last."

"Well, here we are," I replied cheerfully. "Better late than never, right?"

"Absolutely," she agreed.

"So Susan, thanks for meeting us here. I did not want to miss the opportunity with you. As you know we've implemented relationship management strategies in both BD and Operations. We can finally take the time to get it going in Finance," I said, smiling at her obvious excitement."

"I've been told about that," she said. "Our processes have changed too, and I can see that almost everything has started to run around relationships."

"I'm glad you're also seeing the results. It means the strategy is working."

"Where do I fit into this strategy then?" Susan asked.

Scaling With Milestones and Market Insight

"Through scaling. As the Finance Manager, you're meant to keep a good relationship with the customers and maintain a smooth cash flow. There are three important factors in scaling: people, process, and money. We've let the Business Development and Operations teams talk about people and the processes but you're responsible for the money, right?"

"Yes, I am."

"Then I need you to work with all the teams to keep the financial projections accurate. Your projections need to create a balance between winning work and performing the work. It's Steve's headache to win the work and it's Jim's headache to perform the work. Your department is in between the two because they can't deliver to the customer without you, right? You're the one who keeps everyone honest. If a Program Manager is off track in their plan, they need to first be honest with everyone about being off track. Then they need to plan on how they can get back on track. This plan needs to flow to you because everything costs money. If work derails, it'll cost the company money and things may exceed budget.

"It's also your responsibility to monitor the cash flow planning and the timing of payments. It's rare for a client company to pay all your fees upfront, right? Business doesn't work like that. Most clients rely on milestone payments to keep each party accountable. They'll say, 'Hey, we'll only pay you when you complete such a task.' It's common for the company to start these deals with their own money before they get paid for these milestones. Your role is to make sure there is always money in the bank for these deals to be executed before the payment is made for each milestone. If a client misses the timing of these payments, don't hesitate in following it up. Timing is important in business because you're planning your expenditures based on the cash flow. The money has to be in the bank at the right time.

"These milestone payments are important to your department too. That's why we need you to keep a positive relationship with the client, especially their Finance Department. If they're a net 45, do they truly make their payments in that 45 or are they net 30? When the contract is being drafted, you'll be in the contract kickoff meeting where you can make sure that the millstone payments are in the forecast. This way, you can manage the expenses on everything you're paying out."

"And we won't miss the beat on where we're at in our cash projections," Susan added.

"Thank you. I know the Business Development guys are doing a lot of good work. I've met Steve and he is good at what he does, but your team still needs to do a deep analysis of each major task they bring to Operations before each contract kickoff meeting. You'll analyze not just the time it'll take to achieve it but also any of the expenses the company might incur. How do you keep up with the market, Susan?"

She thought about the question for a while before answering, "We often look into the Bureau of Labor Statistics to judge our salaries. I have someone in my department who reports the latest on finance to me."

"Awesome. We need to keep up with the market. Where is the market taking us, right? Is our pricing right? What will the customers now expect from us since it's the new trend in the market? Are we addressing these customers' needs? The last question is one that every department needs to answer but in Finance, we need to know if we're overpricing ourselves to the client.

"Again, it's essential to plan for the efficiency of operations. I do not expect you to deliver cheap services to the client because you want to save expenses. Rather, there are relationships you can leverage to save the company money when performing a deal. You could borrow money to save the company expenses. Can you show me your latest financial forecast?"

"Of course," she said, spinning around her laptop so I could see what was on her screen. She had it open already.

	2020	2021	2022
Total/ Estimated Income	$ 1,424,801	$ 3,263,315	$ 4,316,255
Total/ Estimated Cost	$ 1,245,631	$ 2,807,465	$ 4,125,690
EBIDTA	$ 179,170	$ 455,850	$ 190,565
	Actual		

	2023	2024	2025	2026
Total/ Estimated Income	$ 4,507,601	$ 5,409,121	$ 6,490,945	$ 7,789,134
Total/ Estimated Cost	$ 4,125,690	$ 4,950,828	$ 5,940,993	$ 7,129,192
EBIDTA	$ 381,911	$ 458,293	$ 681,549	$ 817,859
	Forecast			

Fig. Financial Forecast Table

The Projection Puzzle

"Okay, this looks great," I commented after studying it. "Liv, have you had a chance to look at it?"

"Yes," Liv answered.

"Susan, can you tell us how you built this? Liv and I have talked about your finances being flat this year but I noticed that you had a little blip where your income went up while your expenses stayed the same. How did that happen?"

"The expenses were just our usual cost of living," Susan began. "We were able to charge our customers but we didn't hire any new employees and some of our bills were paid so we had no extra expenses. As you can see, the income was only up a couple of percentage points."

"I noticed that you've forecasted the next three years. Talk to me through how you did that."

"Based on the discussion I've had with Liv and the team after your talks with them," she said, "I built the forecast to show twenty percent growth with a similar projection in the course. I've made a few modifications in the cost to show some savings and our bottom line also increased even though we only went up twenty percent each year in three years. Based on this forecast, we should be able to double our net income."

I thought about her words for a minute, running through the pros and cons of this projection in my head. I finally said,

"There are several things you need to consider before drawing out this projection. First, will you be able to integrate this projection into the overall strategy? It sounds like you're only considering the financing aspect. We want to make sure that you've got the top line. Your projections are good but you need to communicate this to the other teams. We need to get the costs and the percentages out there for everyone to understand where they fit into the number. The idea is to set a metric where we can track the cash projections and make sure every department is following them. After all, these employees are responsible for sending you the data that you eventually compile as your financial forecast. By holding them accountable, you're ensuring that their reports are accurate."

"But wait, Brian," Susan cut in. She looked through her notes, paused, and looked up at me, "What if these things don't go according to plan? Finance isn't always linear. Somewhere, there could be an asymmetrical situation. The basics of finance and business, as you know, is to prepare for the unexpected."

Anticipating the Unexpected

"True. Your financial projections will also include provisions for things that are non-linear. If you win a deal and something that's not part of your forecast comes out of the blue, you should have a dynamic system that can capture that and add both revenue and cost to the projection. Unplanned things happen all the time. When they happen, what's your plan for cash shortfalls or shortages? If XYZ Inc., for example, has a problem that makes them ask for an extra thirty days to pay, what's your plan for that? As

I said, timing is important in finance. If the money isn't there when it's supposed to be, what's your backup plan in the financial projection?"

"What should it be?" Susan questioned.

Banking on Relationships

"This is where your relationships start to come in. Your good relationship with the Program Managers and the Business Developers, strengthened by communication and clear metrics setting, is what keeps your projections right. When things don't go according to plan, it's proper relationship management that'll get you out of it too. This time, it can be a good relationship with your banks or financial institutions where you can get loans to keep business running until XYZ Inc. makes their milestone payment."

"How do we maintain a good relationship with the bank?" Liv asked.

"Interview your bank regularly to make sure you're still on the same page with them. Bank policies change. There's nothing that says you have to stay with the same bank as you grow. You might even need to get two banks or more so that each can give you the programs you need. One bank might have better fees for your day-to-day operations while the other has better programs for your operating line. As the Finance officer, Susan, you should keep a good communication line with your banks. You never know when you might need them. When you eventually do, you don't want to be just another name on an email asking for a loan or whatever else you need.

"Sometimes, a bank may not be the best option. In this instance, there's nothing wrong with non-standard financing options like invoice financing or private loans. Keep your mind open."

"Does all this still go into financial projection?" Susan asked.

"Yes. It's your consideration for emergencies. A backup for your backup, if you will. As you're building the financial projection, you need to align the forecast and the finance requirements. If you pick up a task, do you have the cash to completely scale it? Do you have to do short-term finance or a short-term blip to get cash that'll cover any growth?

Risk, Reward and Relationships

"Before considering a loan, it's crucial to assess your bank's lending policies and risk management protocols. Does their policy align with the amount you intend to borrow? Some banks provide an operating line that necessitates the withdrawal of the entire sum. This operating line often serves as a reserve for financial management. However, securing an operating line is already a component of your risk management strategy. It's unnecessary to introduce additional risk to the company by taking out a loan when there are sufficient funds in a savings account. Therefore, ensure the financial blend is appropriate and well-considered.

Repayment Plans

"As you're planning to borrow from a bank or any financial institution as a backup in case of an emergency, make provisions for a repayment plan too. Loans are meant to be repaid. This repayment should not cause cash problems for the company because you still have a payroll that brings in money. The repayment plan needs to be a part of your financing when you're creating the financial projection.

Considerations for Equity

"When you borrow, you want to build equity. One of the things on your balance sheet will be owner's equity, right? It's of utmost importance that you can explain your end goal to whoever you're asking for money. All they will see when they look at the balance sheet is all these new debts the company is picking up. You need to be able to assure them that you understand what your balance sheets say but the new debts all fit into the total plan."

"My team already does that," said Susan.

"Yeah, I'm sure that's not new for you, but here I'm talking about the relationship you need to have with your banks and the lenders. You need honesty and transparency. When you deal with them straightforwardly, you can stay out in front of any problems you have. If they're worried about the new debts you're picking up, assure them you have a plan for them. Any questions?"

Equity, Acquisitions and Organic Expansion

"We've been talking about borrowing," Liv started, "but I've always been uncomfortable with it, whether it's borrowing from a bank or another financial institution. I believe in creating equity instead. Is that such a bad idea?"

"That will be understandable if you're chasing organic growth, like we've been talking about. You need money to grow and continue to grow. If the company is profitable, you'll have capital through organic growth, but you don't know when you might run into an opportunity to acquire another company as part of your growth plan."

"Acquire a company? You mean buy one?" Susan asked incredulously.

"Yes. If there's another company your size or larger, maybe even smaller, you might want to buy it. In other words, finding the money, being more efficient, reorganizing the way you do some things using your ISO and Sigma. You're pursuing organic growth to capture the cash you need for scaling. You need the equity, and it's cheaper to get the equity and buy somebody out than it is to build internally. For example, if I'm a general practitioner company and all of a sudden, I realize I need to improve my medical records section, instead of hiring the IT department that understands medical records, going and buying the software, and paying for it to be established, it might be cheaper to just buy a medical records company and make them part of my company. Before buying a company, there are factors you need to consider as well.

A Sample Check List of Things you have to Consider if you decide to purchase

1. Product or Service
2. Target Market
3. Execution Strategy
4. Management Team
5. Capital Requirement
6. Exit Strategy
7. Terms and Financials
8. Strategic Fit

Fig. Acquisition consideration list

"These are the eight questions I ask before acquiring a company," I continued. "You should ask them too. Does the product or service fit into your strategy? What's the target market? If you eventually buy the company, what is your execution strategy going to be? What kind of management team does the company have? How does the team fit into your company? How would you work together with them? What capital will it take to mine? How do they fit into your exit strategy if you eventually decide to sell the company one day?

"The next thing to consider is the terms and financials. Now, this is an important aspect. How will you buy them? How will you raise the money to buy them? Finally, how do they fit into the current company? What kind of relationship will they have with the present company you run?

"I utilize these eight questions when I'm buying a company but they're not only for my use; they've also valuable to an investor. If you need an investor to fund the company acquisition, these are the questions they will want answers to.

"Another good thing about these questions is that you could use them for any company you want to purchase. It doesn't matter what they sell, produce, or the service they offer. The questions are only concerned about the function of the two companies coming together and what that might look like. In the future, you want these new acquisitions to seamlessly integrate with your company, becoming a natural part of your operations. If that requires you to buy faster machines and create a better process, then that's what you need to do. Will you have to bring on additional capability to ensure this seamless transition? What will the hiring plan look like? What are the benefits of hiring new hands compared to keeping the old hands? These are questions that you have to understand under Mergers and Acquisitions. Maybe one day we'll talk about that. For now, think about your overall strategy as a company and how you will build a relationship with people who will finance the acquisition."

Venture into Partnerships: Angel Funds, VCs and Exit Strategies

"How?" Liv asked.

"I would recommend that you start building a relationship with different people who are in angel funds or venture capital organizations. You need to know what their investing patterns are but you won't know all these from a distance."

"How do I get close to them?" Susan asked.

"Venture capitalists and angels often host small events that your company can attend, allowing you to establish and build relationships with them. This way, when you contact them afterward, it won't be a cold call, as they would already be familiar with you. Some might even offer free advice, depending on the strength of the relationship you've built.

"Angels and VCs have different pros and cons. Angels usually offer small amounts in the early stages and aren't as commonly seen. I've never seen angel funds go beyond $200,000. If you're looking to raise $500,000, you might hit up three or four different angel funds, each possibly throwing in $125,000.

"VCs, on the other hand, are like big money guys hunting for deals. It's uncommon for them to jump in before you hit the $3 to $5 million mark. You hear about VCs when there's news of those massive equity deals, like a $30 million or $500 million deal. VCs typically want a controlling stake or at least a big say. They often ask for a seat on your board to make sure you're spending their money right. An angel fund putting in $25,000 won't demand a board seat, but a VC dropping $5 million will want more say in the game.

"So we have to keep a good relationship with them at all times?" Susan questioned.

"Yes."

"What if we want to get rid of them after they've invested? Maybe we no longer need their involvement after each party has made some money together," Liv asked.

"Every investment plan has an exit strategy. A typical investor would ask you, 'Tell me what you're making today?' before investing. In other words, they want you to tell them the state of your finances and how profitable you are. They'll ask you, 'Based on this money I'm giving you, what do you think the terms in ROI are going to be on it? Is this going to be a five percent-a-year deal for me? Is it ten percent or are we talking about five-times or three-times the return?' Your answer to these questions will make them decide how the payback will happen."

Liv looked confused. "Payback?"

"Your investors need to make their money back and then some before exiting, right? That's why we refer to the exit strategy as an exit/payback strategy. The exit/payback can happen in different ways. It could be that an angel funded your company in the beginning but you needed more money, so you met a VC who gave you the money on the condition that all the angels leave.

"Your exit/payback would happen differently if you used a debt structure to gain your investors. In this case, an angel or a VC gave you money for some interest rate or some milestone. When you've met these milestones, you could decide to pay them off.

"Another exit strategy is when the angel knows that they'll have to leave when the VCs come in. Even a VC can get excited out of the program. Let's say you get to a point where your company is finally stabilized. You could say, 'Let's pay off all the people we owe and just have an organic company again. You could decide to go public and all the VCs will be gone. If they choose to remain, they'll have to become stakeholders. You can only have an equity group, a VC, or an angel if you're private. Once you go public, they're a shareholder, not an owner anymore."

"These are all good strategies," Liv commented.

"Yeah, they are," I said and looked at my watch. "We've come to the end of today's session, Susan. Do you have any questions or is there anything that isn't clear to you?"

Susan paused to look through her notes before replying, "No. Thank you for this, Brian. I'll get back to my team on how we can manage these relationships,"

"Awesome. Thank you for coming.' I stood up and shook her hand before she left.

I sat down and turned to Liv. "Are you not leaving yet?"

"I drove Steve here. He'll bring hell on Earth if I leave without him."

"I'll be coming to your office this Wednesday," I informed her.

"Who do you want to meet, BD or Operations?"

"Everyone. BD, Operations, Finance. I'll meet them all and I'll meet them separately in their offices. I've done my part in integrating relationship management to your strategy. Now, I need you to take off and apply the lessons. When I meet your team next week, it'll be to ask them how they've put all these theoretical talks into real practice."

CHAPTER ELEVEN
THE ART OF ADAPTATION: DRIVING BUSINESS EVOLUTION

Liv's office was my first point of call when I got to the company the following Wednesday. I'd walked through their doors for three months now but the change from the first time I visited continued to amaze me. They serve as evidence of the remarkable results that can be achieved through effective strategy and transparent accountability in business.

While the team's mentality and the company's atmosphere have gone through a lot of changes, Liv's office remained the same."You know I've been thinking about the first day I walked into this place," I said.

Liv looked up at me and smiled, "Me too."

"So, let's go through it all over again. We started with the need for a proper organizational structure and a sound strategy. As the CEO, creating the strategy for the entire company rested on you. How have you worked on implementing relationship management into this strategy?"

Liv sighed before replying, "Well, Brian, I started by making sure everyone now understands that the company is under a strategy with a focused plan. If we wanted to grow, we would have to change some things. I can't remember who said this but someone once said that insanity is doing the same thing over and over and expecting different results."

"Einstein," I answered.

"Yes. To change the results, we had to change the process. Steve was against this change as one would expect. Not every employee wants change after all but he came on board after you confronted him. I had a new strategy put in each department just to remind them that there's Nothing They Kent do…"

"You remember the catchphrase!" I said excitedly.

Liv laughed and continued, "I paid a lot of attention when I was drawing my organizational chart because it was how I could finally put order in my company. The chart allowed me to finally figure out who has the right authority on certain topics. Figuring out this authority matrix also clarified who was responsible for what roles so that metrics could be set and accountability demanded.

"It was important to get these internal affairs right because nothing will be achieved externally unless that internal part is fixed. The company is a machine, as you told me, Brian. Each part needs to do its role flawlessly if growth is to be achieved. If each part does not even know its role, how can we create a good relationship with our clients?"

"When you were refining your organizational structure, did you find any role that wasn't properly defined yet?" I asked.

"When we deep-dived into the chart, we found functions in the company that were not documented appropriately. Those were the AP and AR in the Finance Department. One of Susan's team members used to handle the two but she didn't understand the role well enough. With the integration of the new strategy, the same worker had to start managing relationships with the other departments."

"You've fixed that now?" I inquired.

"Yes. Although we've clarified her role under the new organizational chart, Susan said it'll take some time for the worker to get used to the new status quo," Liv explained.

"That is a lesson you had to learn in practical terms," I commented.

"True," she answered. "We've learned that we are always evolving as a company so there are roles that will be missing in the long run. It's only by constantly monitoring this chart that we can keep up with all the changes inside the company."

"Exactly, Liv. When you find a missing role, you'll have to decide what to do about it. Would you designate someone for it, like you did with Susan's department, or would you hire someone in that department? That is how you clean up the missing pieces one after the other. I have to say you're lucky, too, for having morally upright employees. The office of the AP and AR is a delicate one."

"Susan said as much. We hadn't even included the Program Managers in the financial decision-making process. Improperly filed invoices would have cost us a lot of money. So, we've created a system of crosstalk between Operations and Finance with the Program Managers in between to make sure we have a good system of checks and balances."

"I once had a friend who didn't create a proper checks and balances system in his office. His Finance officer eventually ran off with some of the company's money," I said.

"Oh, dear," Liv exclaimed. "How bad was it?"

"Almost seven figures. The Finance officer was eventually caught but that's not the point. The fact that it happened was irresponsible on the company's part. By creating a proper checks and balances system, just one person should not be able to control the company's finances."

"I'll keep that in mind," she promised.

"Awesome. So, remember to keep your managers accountable too. We've talked about setting clear metrics for these managers and their departments. What goals are they supposed to achieve? How will their goals lead to the company's bigger picture? How do we make sure they are compensated for going beyond the metrics? How would you correct them or the process, if they fall behind?"

Liv sipped her coffee before replying, "We're revising our policies now, Brian. We're getting rid of the old and redundant ones as you suggested. In the new policies we're making, these new metrics are clearly stated. It is my intention that setting these boundaries will decrease conflicts. When everyone knows their role and what is expected of them, I'll rarely have to confront them. Again, the company still needs time to get used to these new policies. It is too much change in a short time."

"I hear you," I agreed. "How about your communication process?"

"Just like I facilitated crosstalk between Finance and Operations, we've worked on creating crosstalk between the other departments. I told each department to give the responsibility of monitoring interdepartmental communication to one employee within their ranks. This way, I want to make sure that monitoring communication is no longer a worker's side hustle. If it's their clearly defined role, it'll be easier for them to monitor the communication. So far, the system has worked out but…"

"You need time to check it out," I helped her complete her sentence.

"Yes," she said, chuckling.

"Okay then, Liv. I think you have your roles dialed down already. While I think about your time issue, I want to talk to Jim and the other managers. When I'm done with them,

I'll circle back to your office so we can talk about what I discovered with them."

I took my notepad and pen as I stood up from my seat. I took a sip from the now cold latte before making my way to Jim's office.

Reviewing and Renewing: Operational Overhaul

This would have been easier if I put everyone in the conference room, I thought. The busy office suddenly went quiet when I opened the door. Jim was bent over another employee's table, probably guiding them through a task. I could also see Peter and Anne on the other side of the room, busy on their computers. I felt cold as soon as I stepped into the room, no doubt because of the air conditioning units that were running at freezing point. With the number of workers in the Operations department and the computers they were using, about fifteen in all, I could understand the reason for the cold temperature.

"Hey, Brian," Jim greeted. "Liv told us to expect you today. Come in, please."

I greeted everyone as I made my way to Jim in the middle of the room. We shook hands and I tactfully moved him into the middle of the room.

"Jim, I need to talk to you but I would rather do that here

instead of the conference room. Will I be making your workers uncomfortable?" I asked.

"Certainly not," he answered. "We can just use Anne's workspace, it's the biggest here. Why don't you wait there while I get Peter?"

The office was back to its busy chatters and keyboard noises. Anne and I greeted one another. Before we could finish exchanging greetings, Jim entered with a chair and Peter followed in tow. We all sat down after getting the pleasantries out of the way.

"So, Jim, I wanted to ask you how things have changed since you started implementing the relationship strategy that Liv created for the company," I said, getting my pen and notepad ready.

"First, I've worked with human resources and implemented the qualification form that you said I can use to decide if a candidate fits into the company's process."

"How's that working out?" I asked.

"Since we're not hiring yet, I've used it to check out the compatibility of our existing staff members here. In the process, we discovered that some of our staff members were not compatible. However, many of them are hardworking and eager to learn so we organized additional training for them in the parts where they were weak. So far, we've conducted training for three workers. The result has been amazing. We have an unprecedented level of efficiency. These workers also feel a debt towards us that they are repaying with loyalty. They know the skills we taught them will remain with them if they decide to leave the company in the future. They also know that we would not have spent so much money training them if we didn't plan to have them in the future. Wait a minute, I told you about this the last time we spoke."

"But not in so much detail," I answered. "Did you find anyone that didn't fit into the new process apart from the three?"

Jim sadly nodded and said, "We did find a candidate that didn't fit. It's a shame because he was good but he was a Microsoft person. Our clients have been insisting on Oracle instead. It's a new trend in the market. We tried to train him like we trained the others but he wasn't responding. I had to have a hard talk with him but he understood."

"Where is he now?"

"He's with Tom."

"Tom? That name sounds familiar."

"Tom, the computer guy who helped us…"

"I remember him now."

"I asked Steve for that favor. I kind of owe him one."

"It sounds as if you two have gotten closer," I smiled.

Jim chuckled and replied, "He's the head of Business Development and I'm the head of Operations. We should have a good relationship, especially now that we're united with our need for the company's growth. We've been able to properly manage our relationship with one another's department through the clear communication procedures we're now implementing."

"How about you, Anne? How are you finding the new developments?" I asked.

"The transparency is the most significant part. We used to be left out of the decision process but now we have an important role."

Peter nodded in agreement and added, "We were used to operational decisions taking place behind our backs but with the contract management that we're now monitoring, nothing gets done without passing through our office. Tell me a better way to make an employee feel important."

We all laughed in agreement.

"The most important part of the process is putting the right person in the right place, right?" I asked.

Jim nodded, "Yes. That's why we had to lose the Microsoft guy. He was a better salesman than an Operations worker. He used to be our wizard in Microsoft tools but we had to lose him. Now, he fits better into Tom's company than ours. We still need more time to get the processes right. We need to continue to review the process and fix whatever mistakes we might have. It also takes time to build a steady relationship with these employees when we haven't bothered to keep one in the past. If we push them too hard to maintain these relationships, it'll become too weird."

"How's your relationship with the clients you're supplying?" I inquired.

"That's another part where we need time. It's easy to build a good relationship with the new clients. They just think that's our usual process and they get used to it. It's tricky with the old clients."

I wrote "More time needed" in my notes and stood up.

"Well, it was great talking to you," I said. "I'll review all you've said and Liv will get back to you. Anne, Peter, I have to say you guys are doing a great job. Keep it up!"

We all shook hands and I left Jim's department for Steve's.

Refining Targets And Reaping Rewards And Business Development

The emptiness was what first hit me when I walked into Business Development. Apart from Steve, and two other workers who were on their phones, the room was almost empty. Judging by the scattered pens and the disorganized table, the owners of the empty tables left the room in a hurry. I walked into Steve's private office where he met me with a handshake.

"Hi, Brian. How are you doing? I've been expecting you," Steve said excitedly.

"I was just in Jim's office. How are you?"

"I should ask how you survived that freezer."

We laughed and he offered me the seat across from him.

"I was just talking to Victor, the gentleman I met at that conference."

"How's it going?" I asked.

"I'll get him," he replied confidently.

"So, how's this new strategy working out for you?"

"You have no idea. I walk into the office with my head held high now. Fifty bids with no wins will bend your head really fast, Brian. Now, it's win after win. Your process is easily scalable too. Look at the Southeastern Contracting for instance. They're one of the companies I met at the party."

"Oh yeah. The ones Liv woke me up to discuss."

"Yeah. Following the MAN, we found their Contracting Officer as our point of entrance into the company. We found her through LinkedIn as you suggested. I had a good conversation with her, we had coffee a few times, and just like that, we drilled into the company. We found the gentleman who is the Budget Manager through her and he linked us up with the end user, Joseph. We're setting up a schedule for him now and we've started to analyze the company so we can know the questions he will want answered before he can choose us. We'll get him too. Now, we've recognized the Budget Manager has a tight grip on the money. The Contracting Officer is with the one with overall approval or authority on deal structure and Joseph has the need. The job is easier when we focus on these three."

"Do you have any other leads you're working on?"

"We're looking at some of the government agencies. We're tracking their spending to see who would need our services. We're also looking for keywords in the federal budget so we can start identifying targets that we can put back into quadrant three. They will be new clients but we will know they have money, so we can now drill into them using the same MAN process," Steve explained.

"Awesome, Steve. That's a good summary," I complimented. "Do you think that the team can now see the value of identifying the customer using the MAN process?"

"Of course they do. When was the last time we've been busy like this? They know the importance of managing these relationships."

"Okay then. About the government contracts, which departments are you really focusing on?"

"You know Liv and I are ex-soldiers. It only makes sense that we're favoring the Department of Defense and the Department of State. We understand their spending habits a bit better. Also, we served with a Sergeant Major in Germany. We spied his name in the right place two days ago so he could be our point of entry but we need more time. That's the only downside to all the targets we're currently refining. I don't want to burden us with too many targets."

"That part is important too. So, you know these two departments have the money to spend on data analysis?"

"Yes, we do. We saw it in their budget. We also have a point of entry. It's only a matter of time."

I jotted "Time" again in my notepad. I stood up and shook Steve's hand. "You're doing a great job, Steve," I complimented him again.

"It's all thanks to you," he answered.

When I left Steve's department, I considered going to the Finance Department but I had just spoken to Susan the week before. I didn't expect her to have any tangible achievement yet. *Time again*, I thought. I decided to go back to Liv's office.

Pillars Of Progress: Education, Stakeholders And Communication

"You're back," she said.

"Yeah," I replied and sat on the sofa. She also joined me.

"So?"

"You have awesome workers. You're a lucky CEO. I expected my notepad to be filled with a lot of recommendations by now but I only have a few."

"Let me hear them, please."

"First, since your team has now refined the functional capabilities needed at each department, we need to come up with a way of continuous education on the business landscape. We've been changing a lot of processes so fast that the employees may not be able to keep up with them. We need every employee who talks to the customers to know what's happening out there in the marketplace. Keeping up with these trends requires continuous education, right?

"I've also been told about how you've changed software to make your service more efficient. Is there going to be a licensing issue in the future? Are there restrictions in that software that could affect your clients? Not only should you know the answer to these questions, your customers should know them too."

Liv wrote in her notepad and nodded her agreement.

"In addition to keeping their knowledge up to date," I continued, "your employees should educate your clients too. If XYZ Inc., still has an old database that will make their work difficult, your employees should be able to inform them about what they're missing out on by not upgrading to the latest database. This is still a part of relationship management, right?

"We should further identify the potential problem that new regulations will bring, especially now that we're adding government clients to our business. Staff education should not be limited to processes and software alone. You need continuous education on regulations too. What was acceptable yesterday may no longer be acceptable the day after. Government institutions will keep tabs on these regulations and so should we, right? We should know enough that the clients can ask us questions about new technologies, new regulations, or new processes."

"Am I supposed to teach all the employees about these? It'll cost a fortune!" Liv countered.

"No, no," I quickly clarified. "Employees should be trained according to what they need to know before they can perform their work effectively. Don't be like the government that is now considering arming IRS officers."

"What do you mean by IRS officers will be armed? They are accountants," Liv said in surprise.

"Exactly my point. Why armed accountants? They are not marksmen. So, focus on teaching your workers what they need to know. They should know their job so well that they can teach it to a five-year-old.

"Now, there are things that we can't teach them because we don't know them yet. In life, there are known unknowns and unknown unknowns. The unknown unknowns mean that we don't know what we just don't know. There are things like that in business that happen without warning. We have no idea they will happen. They just happen and we have to figure them out.

"Not so long ago, there were no smartphones in the world. Then they came into the market and changed things. Susan's financial forecast for the next three years needs to consider the impact technology will have on our strategic plans. Technology evolves every 12 to 24 months and you can be sure that it will affect the way we do business eventually. AI is the new big thing, right? We need to keep a pulse on what's happening in the market so that we can acknowledge these unknown unknowns as they start showing up in our ecosystem."

Liv nodded again.

"After education, you need to find a way to keep up with the stakeholders in your business."

"We don't have shareholders yet," Liv corrected. "We're not yet publicly traded."

“Yeah but for now, I’m referring to your employees and everyone your company touches. Keep good relationships with them all. What’s happening with Susan in Finance? How is Jim carrying on? Is Steve meeting his marks? How satisfied are your customers? These are the stakeholders you need to keep up with. For the stakeholders within your company, that is why we have meetings—weekly, monthly, quarterly, and annually. Anytime you see something change in the company, no matter how small, you should know what it is and how it affects the process. These are the talking points in the meetings. This is where proactive communication comes in. One up, two down,” I concluded.

“Lastly, I want to discuss external stakeholders. You should recognize who your stakeholders truly are and keep up with them. Anything that touches your stakeholders can touch your company. Next the process of staying updated on changes in the business environment. If you’re a small business, stay up with any new information that the Small Business Administration provides. I am not saying take out a small business loan. I am saying that business changes and keeping up with new information about businesses in your industry that are your size and larger helps you drive your business. Proactively communicating with your stakeholders can prevent minor issues from snowballing into major problems that could have been resolved with a simple conversation. I know I have talked a lot about communication, but it truly is key in everything you do in your business.”

“I still remember that,” Liv confirmed.

"Everyone in your team, including you, has asked for more time to properly refine this new strategy and to manage relationships with both new and existing clients. I can see the sense in that so I'll give you 90 days to implement the strategy fully. During this time, we won't exchange emails or phone calls. If you have problems, please think about them and find a way to solve them. The ones you find quite hard should be written down. I'll come back after 90 days to see how far we've come. Is that good with you?" I asked.

"Yes, it is," Liv replied.

"Great. Your time starts today, so let me get out of your hair. Good luck, Liv."

CHAPTER TWELVE
STRATEGIC LEADERSHIP AND DYNAMIC ANALYSIS

Time, the gentleman who is always in a hurry. I had given Liv and her team a 90-day challenge that I was sure they could pull off. We refrained from direct contact during this time, although I would think about the company occasionally. I calmed myself with the assurance that it was in good hands until I could no longer bear the suspense. So, I cheated by following them on their social media accounts. I monitored their positive growth during this time and even I was surprised with the results they were able to achieve. A friend even mentioned their name to me in passing, praising them as the next big thing in Florida. The business world is a small one and word spread very fast here. If you keep a good company that maintains a good relationship, everyone will know. If you have a bad relationship with customers, shareholders, stakeholders, or employees, everyone will know too.

On the final morning, Liv call came in before I could dial her number

"Hi, Liv," I said. "You beat me to it."

"Hi, Brian," she answered with a chuckle. "What time are we meeting tomorrow?"

"Is 11 a.m. okay with your team?"

"I'll make it okay, don't worry. Do you want to meet them individually again?" she asked.

"No, please. Let's meet in the conference room this time."

"Who do you want to meet?"

"Everyone," I said.

The Final Lap

Have you ever met up with a former classmate after graduation? Perhaps they were one of your best friends in high school. You might have read together, studied for tests together, and played games together but you lost contact after graduation. Then you meet them five years later and it seems as if you were shaking hands with a stranger. I felt the same when I walked into Liv's office the next day. The change was evident in the reception area. While Kerry still looked well dressed and as professional as always, the room felt more homely. They had replaced the chairs in the room with more comfortable sofas. Behind Kerry's table was the company's nameplate, printed in gold with a large font. Below the nameplate, they added an assurance for their customers, "Your satisfaction is all the data we need."

"Hi, Brian," Liv called to me. I was so busy checking out the new interior designs that I didn't notice her sitting on one of the sofas.

"Liv, this is awesome," I said.

She laughed and came closer to shake my hand. I stared at the changed woman in front of me and I could hardly recognize her. Gone were the dark circles beneath her eyes and the crease that constant frowning had added to her forehead. She was looking more like the military woman I saw in the picture in her office.

"This is awesome," I repeated.

"Wait until you see this," she said and led me through the door into her office. My eyes caught its left wall when I entered the room.

"Is that…" I asked incredulously.

"Yes, it is," a smiling Liv replied.

"Wow!" I was left speechless, a rare occurrence for me. Bold letters on the wall said: "There is nothing you Kent do."

"This means a lot to me," I said when I finally found my voice.

"I know," Liv agreed. "It's also a good reminder every time I sit in this office. Now, let's go meet the others in the conference room."

The room sprang to life when Liv and I entered. It seemed like everyone wanted to shake my hand at once. At some point, I could no longer keep track of who was shaking my hand and whose greetings I was responding to. Steve was there with Dan and Roy, his sales representatives. Susan also sat next to Jim, who was there with Peter and Anne, his Program Managers. After the handshakes finally ceased, everyone sat round the table and I started.

"Hi everyone. I can wholeheartedly say it is a pleasure to be here with you all again after the short break we had. When I left here three months ago, I promised we would meet after having the time to implement the relationship management strategy into the company processes. I'm sure everyone is bustling with good news to share."

Laughter filled the room, with even Steve throwing his head back in amusement, repeating, "You bet. You bet."

"Well, let's start with Jim. How have you managed your relationship with the workers under your care as well as the clients?"

"We started by enforcing the qualification sheets," Jim began, "Since the last time we spoke, we've hired two new workers in Operations and we used this sheet to consider their hiring process. One of the new workers is in charge of keeping track of the new industrial trends. Any new technology we need to know about or any new development that can affect our business is brought to my notice immediately so that we can educate the other workers about them. The second hire was a Customer Service officer. Their job is to keep us connected with the current customers we have."

"What have you done about your metric and accountability system?" I asked.

"We've created a process where every non-marketing employee who brings us a new client gets a bonus in their next paycheck. One of my Operations workers brought in three developed leads last month alone and we transferred her to Business Development immediately."

"Right butts in the right seat," I thought aloud.

"Yes. Everyone's roles have been clearly defined so there is less friction. Each department and team knows what it is accountable for. In short, it's been a smooth ride throughout this month.

"The company's relationship with employees has significantly improved too. We keep opinion boxes in each department now where everyone can make a complaint anonymously or suggest how they think we can improve. We've also kept a cordial relationship with our clients through that Customer Service officer I talked about. That was how we included a premium package for our clients."

"A premium package?" I asked.

"You know how privacy laws are now big things?" Jim asked. "It turns out that some of our clients had pending court cases because users have accused them of using their data irresponsibly. We didn't know that until we got closer to them. We then decided to offer a new capability where we can help them protect the privacy of their users while still analyzing the data they need. It was a bomb. Completely blew up beyond our expectations."

"We even used it to entice several new clients to fill our fourth quadrant," Steve added.

"This is awesome news. Steve, how is your relationship management going?"

"You should know we got Southeastern Contracting," he bragged.

"You did?" I said in fake surprise. I never doubted it.

"Of course. I got Victor too. The only tricky ones have been the Department of Defense and the Department of State. Bureaucracy is a nightmare, trust me. We drilled in through that entry point but closing the deal has been devilish. We'll get them soon enough.

"As for staff education, I've made sure to bring either Dan or Roy with me every time I had a meeting with a client, especially if we were about to close the deal. Dan closed the deal with Southeastern Contracting—under my able management of course. Roy is about to close another deal for us. So far, we have a hundred percent closing rate with all the leads we're chasing. Business Development is on fire," Steve concluded, beaming with confidence.

"This is great. Susan?" I asked.

"We've opened accounts with two more banks in addition to the two we had before. The four banks have different offers for us and I've been able to maintain a relationship with the management of the four banks. It's a lot of emails and it takes a lot of phone calls but I'm familiar with them all. I have a closer relationship with two of the four. We haven't had a reason to need their help yet but if that time comes, you can be sure that we will have their eyes.

"Steve also introduced me to an angel investor here in Florida. Through his invitations, I've been to several investor parties and I've made friends with many of them. One even invited me to his child's baptism the other day, we've become that friendly. I've met two VCs too. If Jen needs investment today, I won't need to look very far because some of these investors have been pestering me about their need to put their money in the company I talk so much about."

"Well, Liv. Your team has worked a miracle. Awesome job, everyone. Awesome!"

I started to clap and they all joined me. Someone across the table even hollered. When the applause died down, I started to share my notes with them.

Strategic Thinking and Analysis

"You guys have done well but that doesn't mean you should relent in any way. Remember what I said about complacency and how it can become a bad habit if you let it. Let's not get complacent. Instead, remember to focus on the other aspects that require your attention. For instance, the Business Development team should still remember the importance of TRF—Think, Research, and Focus.

"It's the same thing as doing your homework but splitting it up that way should remind you of the steps you need to take before approaching a target, right? Who are the people you need to keep a relationship with? Think about how you want to dig into them. Research and focus on how you can understand them to be the strategic partner they need. Emphasize consideration and research before you act. Don't just approach a potential buyer as a cold call. Know them, understand them, solve their problems, and the doors to their business will be open to you.

The Power of SWOT

"It's something we've been talking about since our first meeting but we just didn't give it a name yet. It means Strength, Weakness, Opportunity, and Threat. What are our strengths as a company? Where are we weak? What opportunities can we capitalize on? What threats do we face in the market? These are the questions that need to be answered by your SWOT. That's why we need an active plan and an updated strategy. We need to play to our strengths and understand our weaknesses. That's how we recognize opportunities that we can capitalize on."

Dan raised his palm and asked, "Can I just jump in with something?"

"Please go ahead," I said.

"I wanted to add that Jim has been helpful in this case. He does a lot of homework on our current customers which has allowed us to bring in new businesses. I'm able to sell better because he keeps a list of the services we provide other customers and our achievements with them. It is therefore easier for me to sell by highlighting that strength to zone in on an opportunity."

"That is a great example, Dan. Your collaboration with Jim is great too because SWOT is multidimensional, right? Before expanding an opportunity, there are two things you're supposed to think about. The first is to go to your Operations department and ask them if they can handle the opportunity you're seeing. Essentially, don't over promise on what you can't deliver. The second thing is to think about the problems you might face while capitalizing on the opportunity. What are the threats you might face? What are the constraints you might run into if you go into that model? What happens then is that you will cultivate new strengths from these new opportunities you find."

"It is a bit confusing for me," Steve owned up.

"Me too," Liv said.

"Okay, let's consider the new capability Jim's department just discovered: offering clients a premium by ensuring their end users' privacy. This can be considered a strength. However, a potential weakness might arise if the region where we intend to expand has regulations that prohibit such data collection practices. This would pose a conflict with the policies of that particular state, turning our strength into a weakness. On the other hand, an opportunity arises when the Operations department identifies a problem their clients are facing through effective relationship management. They said, 'Hey, we see this problem you have and we have a solution but it'll cost you extra because we also will have to work more.' That's capitalizing on an apparent opportunity.

"If a new company comes up all of a sudden with that same privacy offer for your clients, then that's a threat. It's a possible way that you could lose that opportunity, especially if it's a competent competition. It's like when Apple puts out a new phone and people start abandoning the old phones to buy the new ones. When data is the same way, people find a methodology for it. If it all shifts, everyone shifts in the same direction to catch the new thing in the market. So, we can't be caught off guard when a new competitor is in town. If we're expanding our business, we can't ignore the competition that was in that market before us. Do you have any other questions?"

"No," Steve replied.

Securing Finances and Transparency

I turned to Susan. "Given the methodology we've discussed, particularly in terms of your forecasting, the involvement of Program Managers in maintaining checks and balances, and the transparency surrounding the data you're currently acquiring, are you finding that this approach is providing you with improved opportunities and more accurate financial forecasts?"

"Yes," she replied. "We've instituted a process where the PMs now sign off on the invoices and my monthly reports before they reach Liv's table. They check my forecasts to make sure everything there aligns with where they need to be. This has created a transparent system where things that have not been accounted for yet can be captured with Jim's help. The system allows me to refine our future better than before because the crosstalk between the departments helps me to capture all the data I need to make an accurate forecast."

"Are the Program Managers beholden to a certain department?"

Susan wanted to answer but Anne beat her to it. "We evaluate the programs independently," she said. "My style of evaluation is also different from Peter's but we both get the work done efficiently."

"Yeah," Susan continued, "Peter monitors the quarterlies of our clients as well. The reports he submits assist us in predicting where their financials are heading. If there will be any peak or valley in their financial future, we can now predict that. As you can guess, this helps us to make better-informed decisions on variables that tend to change."

"Have you been using it to also know when to walk away from a deal?"

"No, we haven't been using it that way yet. As Steve said, we've been having a hundred percent success rate so far," Susan mentioned.

"Yeah, that's impressive. I just want to remind you that the winning streak won't last forever. Some targets are just dead leads sometimes. Honestly, the desire to push through and not give up is a good thing but we should also know when to just cut ourselves away from a target. It is the art of knowing when to walk away. If it is costing you more money than you originally budgeted, it is time to walk away. If it is not worth the time and energy you expend on it, then walk away. Keep this in mind. Sometimes walking away is the best way to win something.

"I like the way you keep your eyes on changing variables. It's how to ensure a company's longevity. Your change of software when you recognize the new market trend, for example, will keep you ahead of your competition. For the Finance department, putting the changing variables into consideration will make your forecasts more accurate. Have you experienced this?" I asked Susan.

She thought about it for some time. She finally snapped her fingers when she remembered something, "Yes. We noticed that the license of the new software cost more than we thought it would. We renewed the contract for some of these software and they cost more than the previous ones we used."

"Well, Jim, do you need this software to maintain your profitability?"

"Yes, we do," Jim answered.

"Then Susan can only capture the new costs to create a new forecast. Hopefully, we can get the money back. Is there anything else you need help with?"

Everyone looked at one another but no one indicated a new problem. I heaved a huge sigh of relief.

"Then, we're done here. I'll follow up on your growth. When is your next quarterly review?"

"Next week," Liv replied.

"I'll look forward to that. Congratulations everyone!" I stood up and started to clap. Everyone joined me. It went on for a long time and they started to hug one another.

For me, it was a moment of great pride to see the result of what was a lot of work and effort. The happiness of clients when they finally achieve the growth they've always looked for will never get old. Liv turned to me and offered her hand, "I guess this is goodbye then."

"It's not goodbye but see you again," I answered. "We will continue to communicate about the company. If you need any help, reach out to me."

I still receive phone calls and emails from Liv whenever her team hit a snag but that was the last time I stepped into the company. They were eventually named one of the fastest-growing companies in America three months after that last meeting in the conference room. These days, they are finally acting on their expansion dream of reaching Europe.

CHAPTER THIRTEEN

SEE YOU AGAIN

I hope this book has given you the know-how to be able to steer your business ahead using solid relationship management strategies. The struggles we discussed in the book are the same ones many CEOs, owners and managers face—maybe just like you or someone you know, like Liv. Liv represents those many business owners who grapple with the tough call of closing their business within two years of launching. While this book sets out a clear path to progress, it's crucial to keep it real with yourself and your team about where you're at right now.

In my day-to-day work with various industries, I often see leaders struggling with or feeling dissatisfied with their company's performance. They tend to think that having the best product alone guarantees success. "We've got a great product, so people will definitely buy it," is a common sentiment. Similarly, they can't figure out why their proposals don't yield the expected results. They often make excuses to avoid nurturing solid relationships with key stakeholders, hindering their growth.

If you find yourself in this boat, it's time to shift your mindset. These days, many people wrongly equate relationship management with sending short texts or forwarded emails to clients. But building effective relationships goes way beyond these surface-level interactions. If you don't foster strong connections with vendors, buyers, employees and leadership, it's tough to gain support for even the most exceptional products.

I wrote this book with organizational leaders in mind. It encourages taking responsibility for decisions, avoiding blaming the team, and, most importantly, making timely and decisive choices. Remember, you're the captain of your own success!

Building The Business Mindset

Even if I don't leave you with anything else, I want to impress upon you the importance of having a clear business vision. You need to see your business with open eyes, not with rose colored glasses. There is a difference between reality and the situation you are telling yourself is the reality.

To gain a clear perspective on your business, you need to assess the current state of your Finance, Product/Services, and Business Development departments. Understanding where you stand is the first step towards establishing a comprehensive business vision. Are you facing stagnant growth, or are you already sensing potential troubles? Be honest with yourself and avoid seeking false reassurance.

Following this, define your business objectives before taking action. What is the ultimate goal of your efforts? Are you aiming to establish a multinational corporation, or are you content with a local presence? Once you ascertain your current position, you can begin looking towards the future. Consider it akin to troubleshooting a software issue on a MacBook. The logical first step is to reboot the system, as it reverts to a familiar starting point. It's thoughtless to plunge yourself and your team into action without a comprehensive understanding of the larger strategy you'll need to turn things around.

The age-old adage "time is money" rings true here. If you find yourself repeatedly hitting roadblocks due to a lack of clarity on your destination, you're essentially squandering valuable time, ultimately leading to financial losses. Successful business operations rely not only on devising a robust plan but also on ensuring your preparedness to execute that plan effectively.

When you're devising your plan, it's critical to communicate your vision clearly so that your team can play their part. Regardless of your capabilities, you can't manage everything alone. With a team of human workers, errors, conflicts and mistakes are inevitable, but when handled carefully, they can lead to remarkable outcomes. To mitigate such challenges, incorporating accountability, metrics and boundaries is crucial for guiding decision-making processes that align with your business vision. Using an authority matrix can also instill order within your team structure.

Even after assessing your current and desired positions, meaningful change won't occur unless the processes themselves are altered. I ask my clients five key questions:

1. Have you done your initial assessment?
2. Do you have a strategy or plan?
3. Where are you in the implementation?
4. Do you want to do what it takes to fix it?
5. What do your employees say about you?

These five questions help you get your eye on the ball and start building a business mindset.

Once you have the right business mindset, cultivating your leads is the next important step to moving your business forward. Within the book, we've talked about leads and emphasized the importance of client satisfaction and fostering valuable partnerships, alongside your dedicated team, of course.

Making sure your connections are strong leads us to the MAN principle: Money, Authority and Need. Knowing who the MAN is on your client's side can make all the difference in getting those bids locked in. Keep this in mind as a crucial part of managing your relationships and ensuring your bids stay on track even when you're not around. In simpler terms, if you've got a solid plan in place and everyone's clear on who the MAN is on the customer's end, you're more likely to see your bids turn into successful deals rather than falling through.

Goals and Goal Setting

As the one leading the way, it's important to have a clear vision and a plan to make things happen. Each leader has their own style, shaping how they present themselves, build relationships and measure success. The key is to stay focused, set achievable goals and work hard to make them a reality. Remember, when you write down a dream with a deadline, it becomes a goal. Break that goal into steps, and you've got a plan. Put that plan into action, and before you know it, you've made it happen.

Defining Your Goal

Your company's goal should be the backbone of its essential functions. Think of your company's vision as the perfect fit for your goals, like a glove on your hand. The objectives you set should seamlessly align with this overarching vision.

Set your targets beyond what seems immediately achievable. Remember how a child, when taking their first steps, looks ahead, not down at their feet. They're not just thinking about reaching the other side of the room, but maybe even eyeing the kitchen. As they move forward, they find things to hold onto, making their way with determination. Simple, yes, but think about it—the kitchen's where all the food is!

Enlisting the right people to support your goals is crucial. Communicating your objectives clearly to your staff is key in getting them on board with your vision. This support is vital in reaching that first significant milestone.

Strategic Planning

Develop a comprehensive strategy detailing the specific steps, resources and timelines required to achieve your goals. These actions encompass the daily decisions you make, ensuring you hire the right individuals, and sticking to the devised plan. When certain steps in the plan don't yield the expected results, don't hesitate to hit the pause button or slow down to ask crucial questions. Why did this happen? What did we miss? How can we rectify this and get back on track?

Establish a system to monitor and measure your goals effectively. Setting milestones serves as an excellent tool to keep track of your progress. It also allows you to observe whether you're making strides forward or if some adjustments are required. The key is to keep moving, avoiding the stagnant stance of merely longing to be in the kitchen without taking any steps towards it.

Organizational Structure

Establishing the right team is crucial for any organization. Ensuring that every member is placed in an appropriate role and contributing effectively can be the difference between success and stagnation. Here are some key points to consider when building your dream team:

- **Focus on capabilities, not just job descriptions:** Prioritize the capabilities of your team members over sticking strictly to predefined job descriptions. Ensuring each person is in a role that suits their strengths leads to productivity for both you and them. If someone on your Business Development team isn't suited for sales, consider either a different position or parting ways. Helping them find a more fitting job can be a rewarding experience, contributing to a positive reputation. You never know where that might lead.

- **Craft clear job descriptions:** Crafting precise job descriptions will help attract more qualified candidates. A vague description might lead to candidates who, on paper, appear suitable but lack the specific experience required for the job, leading to unrealistic expectations.
- **Attract creative employees:** Look for employees whose skill sets align with your company's strategy. Creative employees don't just think outside the box but also about where the box could be situated. Prioritizing creativity over everything else can be advantageous. Some people might not label themselves as creative, yet in their roles, they consistently strive to find more efficient ways to accomplish tasks, which is a form of creativity.
- **Create an organizational chart:** Don't forget the importance of an organizational chart. It serves as a visual guide for your team, helping everyone understand their place within the company and providing clarity on their reporting lines and team assignments. Also remember every function in the company needs to be captured.

The Wrong Salesperson

Building your dream team isn't always a smooth ride. However, when you have the right people in the right places, nothing can hold you back. Once the team is in place, keeping them motivated and enthusiastic about their work is essential for your business to thrive.

It's crucial to match each team member's strengths with the roles they handle. No one wants to be stuck doing something they don't enjoy or aren't skilled at. It's about finding the perfect fit for everyone on your team, no matter the size of your company.

Dealing with team mismatches isn't easy, but it's a necessary step to get your business back on track. Trying to force someone into a role that isn't right for them doesn't benefit anyone. It's better to address the issue directly rather than let it create more problems down the line. Imagine having an introvert handling client calls or engaging in sales. That's not an ideal scenario, right? They might be better suited to roles that require attention to detail and focus. As the leader, you need to ensure each person on your team is in the right place.

If you find yourself in this situation, understanding why someone isn't fitting in is key. Was it a hiring mistake or an issue with the employee's approach? Once you identify the root cause you can get started on finding a solution that works for everyone.

If you find someone is in the wrong role, you'll need to have an open conversation with them about the issue and to discuss potential solutions. You might not resolve everything immediately, but it shows that you care and are willing to work toward a solution together. If you encourage open communication among your team members, it creates a work environment where everyone feels heard and valued is crucial for fostering a positive and productive team dynamic.

Accountability

As a leader, it's crucial to take decisive action in holding both yourself and your team accountable. Avoid getting bogged down in indecision; remember that not making a timely decision is a decision in itself, and you are ultimately relinquishing control of success or failure to chance. Accountability as a leader can take many forms, including:

- Cultivating strong relationships and considering all the people surrounding you from every angle.
- Eliminating ineffective or unnecessary processes and policies that hinder progress.
- Encouraging individuals to utilize their time efficiently and contribute to the overarching vision.
- Evaluating whether certain individuals who exploit the system have a place in your organization.

Remember, you are building a successful future, not a daycare for adults. Lead with conviction!

Most people simply want to know the direction the company is heading, and trust me, they will rise to the occasion if they feel supported and that you have their backs.

In order to hold your team accountable for their work, you will need to:

- Establish clear metrics for employees to follow, providing them with guidelines and boundaries for their tasks.
- Ensure that all team members have a comprehensive understanding of their expected responsibilities and objectives.
- Provide employees with tangible goals to meet, fostering a sense of accountability and purpose in their work.
- Use these metrics as a basis for necessary and sometimes challenging conversations, reinforcing the importance of meeting set expectations.
- Prioritize mutual agreement on these metrics, allowing employees to communicate any issues they face in meeting the requirements for timely evaluation and resolution.

Lastly, you need to recognize that every business thrives on people and processes. Familiarize yourself with both within your organization so that when things don't go as planned, you have trustworthy team members and reliable processes to rely on for getting things back on track.

Effective Management to Aid Growth

If you're looking to grow your company, keeping it in check through effective risk management is key. It's the cornerstone that helps you stay on track and ensures your business continues to thrive. Taking a proactive approach to risk management is crucial. It's not just about fixing issues after they arise; it's about foreseeing areas for improvement before they even become problems, especially when aiming for ISO certification.

If you're a manager, you need to analyze and manage risks according to the capability of the team and based on the product or services they are providing. No matter if it is Business Development or Operations, knowing the capabilities of your team is essential in bringing a solid growth plan and that shows the possible risks to overcome and paving the way for delivering.

Workload Optimization

Workload optimization is a principle that is used to decide the role of every position in a department. Some roles may require more than one person to do the job. When you are a small business, for instance, everyone wears several hats because there are fewer people to fulfill the necessary roles. The Finance officer could be the AP/AR and a dozen other roles. In a case such as this, being cognizant of their duties and what is expected can help the person figure out all their roles.

Overloading your employees with excessive tasks does not turn out well in the long run. This is where a good job description and good communication comes into play. By overloading your employees, they are always busy working for the company without taking a time out. If your employees are at critical mass and burnout, you will not get one hundred percent from them and you may end up feeling like you are herding cats rather than cows.

Maintaining a healthy work-life balance for your employees will allow them to perform at their best. For sure, there will be times when you need to push them to accomplish a set mission but this needs to be an occasional development rather than normalcy. Many people feel the need to overwork for a variety of reasons; most entrepreneurs find it hard to keep this balance because they enjoy what they do. Some husbands and wives who start a company together cannot keep this balance because their business is like a child to them. As the business owner, you need to stop and take time to evaluate why a situation is happening before responding and help your employees to do the same—be the example.

Effective Communication

The importance of effective communication can't be stressed enough. Good communication is vital to every business so clear communication channels need to be established with employees to fosters transparency, intra-departmental understanding, and inter-departmental understanding.

Clear communication will help you to be realistic with time allocation for tasks. With the input from your managers and the employees, you can find a time balance that will prevent rushed outcomes while keeping employees on their feet. Your employees need to know that it is better to deliver quality work than to take on more jobs in order to appear eager to help. Rushed work does not end well eventually.

Your confidence in their ability to meet timelines and deliver quality work should further reflect your leadership mentality and encourage them to follow the instructions you leave them. After all, setting expectations by giving them goals and realistic timelines for quality work will be a win-win situation; the employees will be more comfortable with their roles and your work will be done better.

The Four Quadrants

The Four Quadrants, discussed in Chapters 6,7, and 8, are a powerful tools that require a comprehensive understanding of your customers. Without this critical insight, the process might seem daunting, but with some time and effort, you can successfully apply the Four Quadrants to all your clients and make significant progress.

Don't forget to establish a proper authority matrix, as we previously discussed in chapter 2. Remember, identifying the key decision-makers is crucial. For instance, while the junior engineers might appreciate your presentations, they might not be the key players in the company. Always keep in mind the MAN principle: Money, Authority, Need. Place each customer and their capabilities in the quadrants and then work on establishing your MAN. If you already have a good grasp of the MAN and the Four Quadrants, great! If not, go back and reread chapter 6, take the time to gather the necessary information and proceed from there.

Finance and Venture Capital

A business can't be run without money, no matter how good your plans are or how well you implement your strategies. Money is often needed for projects and deals, but raising funds isn't always the only solution. Sometimes, all you need to do is find smarter ways to spend the company's money. Ask yourself:

- In what ways can you save money to invest in other projects?
- Is the deal you want to spend so much money on worth it?
- Can you restructure the deal to save your money ?
- Can you save money by leasing equipment rather than buying?
- Is it better to outsource your marketing until you can afford to hire an in-house marketer?

Cost management is a vital aspect of fundraising to ensure resources are allocated wisely.

Fundraising Strategy

When your cost-saving strategies no longer work, it's time to consider how to raise additional funds. Rapid growth may require more than just cost-cutting to finance your endeavors. When this happens, you need to have a discussion about how you plan to get money to finance your deals. Do you want your business to be financed by angels? Would you prefer VCs? You should learn about each source of financing, the advantages and disadvantages, and how these can align with your strategy. Find out about who you're inviting to invest in your company so you don't end up giving away the farm.

Investors, whether angels or VCs, won't invest in your business unless they see the potential for profit. You'll need to persuasively demonstrate your ability to generate returns on their investment. They are likely to ask you eight specific questions when you present your business to them. These questions are thoroughly covered in Chapter 10.

Target Market Refinement

Target market refinement means regularly adjusting and tweaking the way you identify and understand the people you want to sell your stuff to. It's about keeping an eye on what your customers want and making sure your products or services match up with their needs. Your target market might include government agencies, non-governmental organizations, public companies, or women-centric businesses. However, simply defining your target market isn't enough; it needs continual refinement to align with your business objectives. As people's preferences are constantly evolving, especially in the digital age, your business goals must keep pace with these changes.

Understanding your target market helps you identify your ideal customer, and managing this relationship effectively sets you apart from competitors. Your product or service should cater to the needs and preferences of this ideal customer. However, successful relationship management with your customers hinges on a well-structured company. Without a clear organizational structure, it's challenging to address your customers' needs effectively.

A stable business structure enables your company to remain adaptable and responsive to market changes. Each department must focus on its responsibilities, ensuring that any changes in the market affecting your processes, products, or clients are promptly noticed and addressed. When market changes do impact your business, continuous refinement becomes necessary, whether due to government policy changes, software upgrades, or evolving customer expectations.

Overcoming Obstacles

Good communication, as we've discussed, is the backbone of every successful company. Mastering effective communication techniques is like unlocking the key to success. Don't forget the 2/2/1 method and use your two eyes, two ears, and one mouth wisely!

To tackle hurdles, you've got to set up clear communication channels. A lot of big misunderstandings actually stem from a breakdown in communication. So, before you head into any meeting, make sure you've got your thoughts in order, but don't forget to really listen and understand the other side before you jump in.

Encouraging open and honest conversations is the way to go when it comes to dealing with problems directly. Avoid letting things brew and bubble over because that's never fun, and it usually makes things worse. Whether you're dealing with clients or your own team, making sure everyone's got a chance to speak their mind is key.

Keep those lines of communication open regularly so you're in the loop about what's happening and what might trip you up. I used to have a morning huddle with my team, and even though some weren't thrilled about it, it really helped us get on the same page. Being open with your team encourages them to step up and be part of the solution, and that's how you build a solid dream team.

Creating an environment where people can freely talk about their concerns and brainstorm solutions is crucial. No question is ever a dumb one, so make sure your team knows that. You'd be surprised how even the quietest person in the room might have the best idea. Everyone's voice matters, no matter their title.

Encouraging teamwork and group problem-solving should be a natural part of how your company operates. It's easy to read about it in books, but actually doing it makes all the difference. Imagine seeing your team working together like a well-oiled machine—now, that's something!

And always remember to ask your team for their input. Getting their perspective on the hurdles you're facing can give you fresh insights and solutions. You might have to sift through a few wild ideas, but sometimes, those are the ones that work like magic. So if there's an obstacle, there's definitely a way around it—and we want that way to be a good one.

Input and feedback

To build a solid team, it's important to keep encouraging everyone to work together and solve problems as a group whenever you can. You might have come across this idea in self-help books, but the key is actually putting it into practice.

Ask your team for their thoughts on how to tackle challenges and come up with solutions. One way to do this is to have everyone bring their own ideas to the table. While not all suggestions may work, you could find a valuable one among them. Just remember, where there's a problem, there's usually a way to solve it, and we want that solution to be a positive one.

Living Your Best Life

You can do it! Whether your goal is to own a company or lead a team, it all starts with mastering the basics. Not every idea needs to be groundbreaking; success often stems from mastering the fundamentals. Getting the basics right increases your chances of success, but it's crucial to remember that not every decision will be a perfect one. Thus, you must ensure that even when mistakes happen, they are not catastrophic.

Think of it as hitting singles in a baseball game; with consistent effort, home runs will eventually come your way. Keep in mind that if it were easy, everyone would be doing it. It's normal to stumble along the way, but the key is to stay focused. If you've identified a problem that needs fixing or have an idea to pursue, keep at it. If this is genuinely your dream, give it your all, ensure a solid start, and most importantly, enjoy the journey.

As you progress toward success, strive to bring others up with you. Your life's mission should be fulfilling, so that even during challenging times, you have the motivation to persist rather than throw in the towel. When you do achieve success, take the time to celebrate, recharge and set your sights on even loftier goals. This might not necessarily mean starting a second company; it could involve spending more time traveling with family or giving back to others. Always remember, it's your life to live, so strive to be the best version of yourself!

Self Evaluation

Are you ready to Make the Leap? Review the questions below and answer them honestly. Then after reading the book in 30 days come back to this assessment and see where you have come.

1. What kind of leader am I or what kind of entrepreneur am I?
2. Am I the leader, the entrepreneur, the manager, or the supporting staff?
3. Am I capable of being that manager? Am I making decisions when and how they need to be made?
4. How does my team see me? Can I empathize? Will my personality let me learn my surroundings? Am I continuing to build relationships for success?

As the author of this book and consulting to many leaders, I still evaluate myself routinely. How can I get better? These simple questions are for you to evaluate from your perspective the current situation.

More Books From PERFECT PUBLISHING

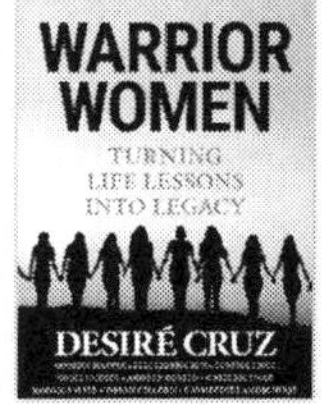

www.PerfectPublishing.com

More Books From PERFECT PUBLISHING

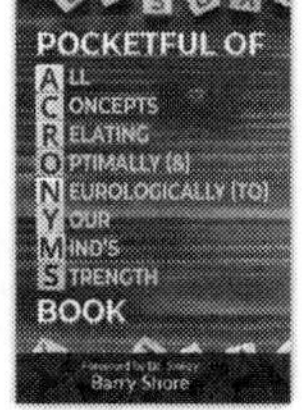

www.PerfectPublishing.com

Made in the USA
Columbia, SC
09 May 2025

57638508R00176